John Churton Collins

Shakspere's Predecessors in the English Drama

John Churton Collins

Shakspere's Predecessors in the English Drama

ISBN/EAN: 9783337342227

Printed in Europe, USA, Canada, Australia, Japan

Cover: Foto ©Thomas Meinert / pixelio.de

More available books at **www.hansebooks.com**

by exhibiting to him a whole host of such blemishes, but we think that the faults of the Margin, to which we have directed attention, are in themselves a sufficient appeal to his common sense.

To the Hebrew scholar we could have appealed by calling his attention, as others have done, to passages which the Revisers have left untouched, where a slight emendation would have been justifiable. We could in fact have shown, had our space permitted, that the Committee, notwithstanding the excellent scholarship of many of its members, has yet been unable to produce a version which is entitled to take the place of the Authorized translation.

With all our gratitude to the Revisers for their labours, we cannot congratulate them on the result. We believe that we have suggested the right cause of their failure, but we cannot dismiss the foregoing remarks without the frank avowal, that our prevailing sentiment in studying the Revised Version of the Old Testament has been one of utter perplexity. All is mystery here. Why is the Margin the worst part of the book? Why do we find so much that, to a thoughtful reader, suggests at first glance views which probably almost every member of the Committee would shrink from, namely views which seem adverse to all Messianic interpretation?

But we are unwilling to take leave of the Revisers with words of censure. We frankly admit the justice of what they claim for themselves and the American Company, that they have been actuated by ' a sincere desire to give to modern readers a faithful representation of the meaning of the original documents;' and we desire to say of them what we said of the Revisers of the New Testament, that their work bears marks of conscientious labour which those only can fully appreciate who have made the same province of study to some extent their own.

- - -

ART. II.—*Shakspere's Predecessors in the English Drama.* By
John Addington Symonds. London, 1884.

THIS volume has more than one important claim to serious
consideration. It is the first instalment of what promises
to be the most voluminous history of our national dráma which
has yet been attempted. As a composition and as a contribution to literary criticism it appears to us, and we have little
doubt that it will appear to Posterity, to mark with singular
precision one of the most curious crises through which our
literature has ever passed. Its author has been long known to
the world as an accomplished and industrious man of letters,
and in undertaking the present work he would seem to have
undertaken a work for which he was peculiarly well qualified.
It has been, he tells us, for many years in his thoughts. It was
commenced nearly a quarter of a century ago; and though its
composition has been suspended, it has, if we may judge from
Mr. Symonds's principal publications, been suspended for
studies which must assuredly have formed an excellent training
for the task which he now resumes. Nor is this all. We have
no wish to speak disparagingly of the historians of English
literature, but it must, we fear, be admitted that they have as
a class been deficient in that wide and liberal culture—that
scholarly familiarity with the classics of other ages and of other
tongues—which constitutes the chief difference between literary
historians of the first and literary historians of the second order.
It is this which has given us many Chalmers but few Hallams,—
much that will satisfy those who seek to be informed, little that
will satisfy those who seek to be enlightened; and it is this
which places the histories of English literature now current
among us so immeasurably below the work of M. Taine. But
assuredly no deficiency on the score of literary attainments and
literary culture can be imputed to Mr. Symonds. His Essays
on the Greek Poets are a sufficient proof of his acquirements as
a scholar. His study of Dante, and his five stout volumes on
the Renaissance in Italy, display an acquaintance with the
literature and history of that country such as probably no
Englishman since Roscoe has possessed. With the poetry and
criticism of Germany and France he appears to be equally
conversant. He has sought fame as a poet, as a translator, as
a critic of the fine arts, and in each of these characters he has
distinguished himself. The appearance, therefore, of such a
work as the present, by so eminent and so accomplished a writer,
cannot but be regarded as an event of importance. It is writers
like Mr. Symonds who fix the standard of literary achievement.

What

What they do has the force of example; what they neglect to do is drawn into precedent. The quality of the work produced by them determinates the quality of the work produced by many others. A bad book is its own antidote; a superlatively good book appeals to few; but a book which is not too defective to be called excellent, and not too excellent to become popular, exercises an influence on literary activity which it is scarcely possible to over-estimate. And of such a character is the volume before us.

We have explained our reasons for attaching particular importance to it, and Mr. Symonds will, we hope, forgive us for commenting freely on what appear to us to be its chief blemishes. It is our duty to say then that there is much in this volume which will, we fear, be of ill-precedent in the future. What we expected, and what we felt we had a right to expect in so ambitious a work, were some indications of the 'meditatio et labor in posterum valescentes,' something that smacked, as the ancient critics would put it, of the file and the lamp. What we found was, we regret to say, every indication of precipitous haste, a style which where it differs from the style of the daily journals differs for the worse—florid, yet commonplace; full of impurities; inordinately, nay, incredibly diffuse and pleonastic; a narrative clogged with endless repetitions, without symmetry, without proportion. To go no further than the opening chapter. Mr. Symonds there observes that Elizabethan art culminated in Shakspeare. Such a remark was assuredly neither very new nor very profound, but it is repeated no less than eight times in almost as many pages. First it appears simply as 'In Shakspeare the art of sixteenth-century England was completed and accomplished.' Then it reappears as 'In Shakspeare we have the culmination of dramatic art in England.' Next it assumes the form of 'Shakspeare represents the dramatic art in its fulness.' Again it presents itself as 'Shakspeare forms a focus for all the rays of dramatic light which had emerged before his time.' On the next page 'Shakspeare is the keystone of the arch.' A few lines afterwards, 'Shakspeare's greatness consists in bringing the type established by his predecessors to artistic fulness.' A few lines before, 'It (the drama) reaches that accomplishment in Shakspeare's art which enthrals attention.' Then again it starts up as 'Shakspeare realized the previous efforts of the English genius to form a drama, and perfected the type.' A not less glaring illustration of the same unhappy peculiarity of Mr. Symonds' style will be found in the chapter on Marlowe: 'The leading motive which pervades Marlowe's poetry may be defined

z 2   as

as L'Amour de l'Impossible.' This is the text, and through twenty-three octavo pages is the remark repeated and illustrated, illustrated and repeated, till the iteration becomes almost maddening. Some portions of the work bear the appearance of having been contributions to periodical literature, which Mr. Symonds has, without revising, and without adapting to the purposes of his history, forced to do service as sections of a continuous narrative. This is always a dangerous experiment, and it has certainly not succeeded in Mr. Symonds' case. A moment's reflection would, for example, have shown him the ludicrous impropriety of prefacing his account of Marlowe with a sketch of the history of the Drama, when a history of the drama had been the subject of the preceding five hundred and eighty-four pages.

To the same inconsiderate haste are no doubt to be attributed the many inaccuracies of statement which deform the work. On page 207 he makes the astounding assertion, that 'in 1566 Literature hardly existed, and that the study of the Classics was confined to a few scholars.' It would be impossible to conceive a description more erroneous and distorted than the description which Mr. Symonds gives, in the second chapter, of the world of Elizabeth. What he says of its intellectual characteristics will apply only to the dramatists, and will even then require to be greatly modified. What he says of its social characteristics is true only of one or two phases of its many-sided life. We can hardly suppose that Mr. Symonds is imperfectly versed either in the dramas of Æschylus or in the dramas of Greene. Yet when he tells us that Æschylus has scarcely any moral precepts capable of isolation from the dramatic context, and that Greene's blank verse betrays the manner of the couplet, he certainly forces us to suspect the sufficiency of his knowledge. What is of course true is that γνῶμαι are far less frequent in Æschylus than in Euripides, and that in Greene's earlier style the blank verse is, as Mr. Symonds describes, constructed on the model of the couplet ; but, for all that, the plays of Æschylus abound in γνῶμαι, and Greene's earlier blank verse is not his later and characteristic blank verse, which is by no means constructed on the model of the couplet. Equally loose and equally untrue is the assertion, that Lyly discovered Euphuism. We are surprised that a scholar like Mr. Symonds should not have known that it would be as erroneous to ascribe to the author of ' Euphues ' the discovery of Euphuism, as it would be ascribe to the author of ' Samson Agonistes ' the discovery of the machinery of the Classical drama ; or to the author of the second book of the ' Novum Organon ' the discovery of wit. Euphuism is in
many

many of its characteristic features as old as Ovid. Even when fully developed,—that is to say in the form which it assumed in Lyly's romance—it had been long before the world, and had Mr. Symonds taken the trouble to glance at the books most in vogue when 'Euphues' was in course of composition, he would have seen that Lyly, so far from setting, was simply following a fashion. Has Mr. Symonds never inspected North's version of Guevara's ' Dial of Princes,' George Pettie's ' Petite Palace of Pettie,' and Castiglione's ' Il Cortegiano'?

Nor is Mr. Symonds more sound in his generalizations on the spirit of the Elizabethan drama. Nothing can be less felicitous than his remark, that that drama is draped with ' a tragic pall of deep Teutonic meditative melancholy,' and nothing can be more unsatisfactory than the evidence adduced by him in support of the remark. It consists of some thirty quotations selected from the speeches of characters who, figuring in tragic scenes, are simply, in obedience to dramatic propriety, expressing themselves in dramatic language. On Mr. Symonds' principle it would be the easiest thing in the world to prove that the distinguishing feature of the Homeric poems is their cynical pessimism, that the distinguishing feature of Chaucer's poetry is its pensive sentimentalism, and that what chiefly characterizes the poetry of Sophocles and Milton is its audacious impiety. What it was incumbent on Mr. Symonds to show was not that such passages as he refers to occur, but that they occur with obtrusive frequency. True it is that there is an undue preponderance of meditative melancholy in the dramas of Webster, Marston, Tourneur and Ford, but this school was only one out of many ; it is confessedly not a representative school, and its productions form but a small portion of the literature on which Mr. Symonds is generalizing. For every play which would give some colour to his remark, there are fifty to which it would not be applicable. The truth is that there is no drama in the world in which the mixture of the serious and humorous is so happily tempered, and which reflects so faithfully the normal conditions of normal humanity.

But these are trifles. We have now to animadvert on blemishes in Mr. Symonds's work of a much more serious character. Within the last few years there has sprung up a school of writers, the appearance of which at a certain period in the history of every literature seems to be inevitable. The characteristics of this school have been the same in all ages. They have indeed been delineated and ridiculed by succeeding generations of critics, by Quintilian and Petronius among the Romans, by Dionysius and Longinus among the Greeks ;
Boileau

Boileau and Voltaire covered them with contempt in France, Cascales and Ignacio de Luzàn held them up to the scorn of Spain, and they were the detestation of Alfieri in Italy. These characteristics resolve themselves into morbid peculiarities of style, and into morbid peculiarities of opinion and sentiment. In the writings of purer schools, style may be compared to a mirror. In the writings of this school it resembles a kaleidoscope. Its property is not to reflect, but to refract and distort ; not to convey thought in the simplicity of its original conception, but to decompose it into fantastic shapes. With them the art of expression is simply the art of making common ideas assume uncommon forms, or in other words the art of simulating originality and eloquence. No senses lend themselves so readily to deception as hearing and sight. The strongest eye if dazzled cannot discern ; the nicest ear if stunned cannot distinguish. And what glare and tumult are to the eye and ear, that in the hands of these writers is language to the mind. Their diction is all blaze and glitter. It has sometimes the effect of spangles dangled in the sun, and sometimes the effect of flame radiating from burnished metal. Its glancing flash baffles ; its unrelieved glare blinds.

The process by which these effects are produced is easily analyzed. In the first place, the phraseology of these writers is selected almost exclusively from the phraseology of poetry. It consists mainly of metaphors. They reason in metaphors, they define in metaphors, they reflect in metaphors, and the metaphors in which they most delight are such as would, even in the enthusiasm of the dithyramb, be used sparingly. Not less characteristic is their habitual employment of hyperbole. Whatever is said, is conveyed in language which reaches the extreme limits of expression. Whatever is described, is described in terms which exhaust the resources of rhetoric. Thus they have no energy in reserve ; when eloquence is appropriate, it has already palled ; when it is necessary to be impressive, the force of impressiveness is spent. They have emphasized till emphasis has ceased to appeal. They have stimulated till stimulants have lost their efficacy. Closely allied with this peculiarity, or to speak more accurately, one of the many phrases assumed by it is the affectation of novel and striking expressions. It was said of Augustus that he avoided as a rock a word not sanctioned by popular usage. It may be said of these writers that what popular usage sanctions it is their chief aim to shun. Thus their diction teems with outlandish words which are sometimes coined and sometimes revived. Thus every eccentricity of collocation and combination in the repertory of vicious rhetoric is
assiduously

assiduously cultivated by them. They out-Ossian Ossian in the tumid extravagance of their epithets and turns. They out-Pindar Pindar in the vehement audacity of their figures. Now we are glutted with what Petronius calls 'honey pellets of sweetened words,' and now we are dazzled with expressions which, to adopt Smith's ingenious mistranslation of a phrase in Longinus, do not shine like stars, but glare like meteors. Everywhere it is the same,—an attempt to produce finer bread than is made of flour, till, like the slave in Horace, nauseated with sweetmeats we long for loaves.

In former times this style, we are speaking of course of prose, was as a rule confined to oratory and history, where, though ridiculous and pernicious, it was not without a certain propriety. In our time it has invaded criticism where it is simply intolerable. The founder and leader of the school of criticism which has adopted it is Mr. Swinburne. Of those brilliant compositions which will, we doubt not, make the name of Mr. Swinburne imperishable, this is not the place to speak. We will only say that what is excellent in his work has no more appreciative, no more hearty admirers than ourselves. But, unhappily, Mr. Swinburne is not content to confine himself to the art in which he excels. His critical writings are now almost as voluminous as his poetry ; and as a prose-writer and critic we believe him to have been guilty of greater absurdities and to have done more mischief than any writer of equal eminence who has ever lived. With the examples of Goethe and Coleridge before us, it would be impossible to accept without reservation the remark of Plato, that those who are most successful in exhibiting the principles of poetry in practice are the least competent to interpret and discuss them—in other words, that the best poets are the worst critics. But assuredly no such reservation is possible in the case of Mr. Swinburne. Of the intellectual qualifications indispensable to a critic he has, with the exception of a powerful and accurate memory, literally none. His judgment is the sport sometimes of his emotions and sometimes of his imagination ; and what is in men of normal temper the process of reflection, is in him the process of imagination operating on emotion, and of emotion reacting on imagination. A work of art has the same effect on him as objects fraught with hateful or delightful associations have on persons of sensitive memories. The mind dwells not on the objects themselves, but what is accidentally recalled or accidentally suggested by them, and nothing is but what is not. Criticism is with him neither a process of analysis nor a process of interpretation, but simple fiction. What seem to be Mr. Swinburne's convictions are

merely

merely his temporary impressions. What he sees in one light in one mood, he sees in another light in another mood. He is, in truth, the very Zimri of criticism, as inconsistent as he is intemperate, as dogmatic as he is whimsical. Indeed, the words in which Dryden paints Buckingham admirably describe him :—

> ' Praising and railing are his usual themes,
> And both to show his judgment in extremes ;
> So over-violent or over-civil,
> That every man with him is God or Devil.'

He is at once the most ferocious of iconoclasts and the most abject of idolaters. In a writer who has been so fortunate as to become the object of his capricious homage, he can find nothing to censure ; in a writer who has had the misfortune to become the object of his equally capricious hostility, he can find nothing to praise. The very qualities, for example, which attract him in Fletcher, repel him in Euripides. He overwhelms Byron with ribald abuse for precisely the same qualities which in Victor Hugo elicit from him the most fulsome eulogy. To exalt Collins, he absurdly depreciates Gray. To degrade Wordsworth, he ridiculously overrates Keats. But it is when dealing with the poets who are the objects of Mr. Symonds's volume that his opinions become most preposterous. The very name of Marlowe appears to have the power of completely subjugating his reason. He speaks of him in terms which a writer who weighed words would scarcely employ, without qualification, when speaking of the greatest names in all poetry. Indeed, he boldly says that, in his opinion, there are not above two or three poets in the whole compass of literature who can be set above Marlowe ; 'and if,' he adds, ' Marlowe's country should ever bear men worthy to raise a statue or a monument to his memory, he should stand before them with the head and eyes of an Apollo.'—But what follows is really too absurd to transcribe. Declamatory eulogy, unsupported by particular references and particular quotations, is not easily brought to the proof. It is fortunate, therefore, that Mr. Swinburne has occasionally, at least, condescended to illustrate his criticisms. In the first part of Marlowe's ' Tamburlaine' occur these lines :—

> ' If all the pens that ever poets held
> Had fed the feeling of their master's thoughts,
> And every sweetness that inspir'd their hearts,
> Their minds and muses on admirèd themes,
> If all the heavenly quintessence they still
> From their immortal flowers of poesy,
> Wherein, as in a mirror, we perceive
> The highest reaches of a human wit.

If

If these had made one poem's period,
And all combin'd in beauty's worthiness,
Yet should there hover in their restless heads
One thought, one grace, one wonder at the least
Which into words no virtue can digest.'

Our readers will probably agree with us that this is a fine passage, but that, fine though it is, it is in no way superior to dozens of others in Marlowe's Plays and to hundreds of others in the Elizabethan Dramas. In Mr. Swinburne's judgment—we give his very words—it is ' perhaps the noblest passage in the literature of the world.' After this it is not surprising to find him placing the satire of Nash side by side with the satire of Swift.

In these ludicrous vagaries of opinion we are glad to see that Mr. Symonds has not followed his master ; but of all the most offensive characteristics of Mr. Swinburne's style, he is, we regret to say, only too faithful an imitator. In some cases he has even gone beyond him. We doubt whether even Mr. Swinburne would have spoken of crudities of composition as ' the very parbreak of a youthful poet's indigestion ; ' or would so far have lost himself in figurative imagery as to describe a drama as ' an asp, short, ash-coloured, poison-fanged, blunt-headed, abrupt in movement, hissing and wriggling through the sands of human misery ; ' or would have represented a dramatist ' stabbing the metal plate on which he works, drowning it in *aqua fortis* till it froths ; ' or would have spoken of ' the lust for the impossible being injected like a molten fluid into all Marlowe's eminent dramatic personalities.'

There is scarcely a page in Mr. Symonds's work which is not deformed with the offensive jargon of his master. The ' carnal' element in Marlowe's genius is ' a sensuality which lends a grip to Belial on the heartstrings of the lust.' Helen's kisses are ' kisses hot as sops of flaming fire.' Marlowe's ' Hero and Leander ' is ' that divinest dithyramb in praise of sensual beauty in which the poet moves in a hyperuranian region, from which he contemplates with eyes of equal admiration the species of terrestrial loveliness.' Occasionally we have such unmeaning expressions as ' the adamantine declamation of Ford,' and the ' torrid splendour of De Quincey's rhetoric.' It may be doubted whether metaphorical extravagance ever went further than in the following sentence : ' When he sees her corpse ' — Mr. Symonds is describing the famous scene where, in Webster's ' Duchess of Malfi,' Ferdinand is standing over the body of his murdered sister—' his fancy, set on flame already by the fury of his hatred, becomes a Hell, which burns the image of her calm pale forehead on his reeling brain.'

And

And now our ungrateful task is concluded. We have so
much sympathy with Mr. Symonds' studies, we are so sensible
of his distinguished services to history and literature, and we
have found so much that is excellent in the present volume,
that had we consulted inclination only, we should have re-
frained from everything bearing the appearance of adverse
criticism. But the duty imposed on us as critics is, we feel,
imperative, and that duty would be ill-performed if we did not
raise our voice against innovations which we believe to be
vicious and mischievous. That the style which we have been
discussing is a fashion, and will, like other fashions, pass away,
we have no doubt. What is to be deeply regretted is that it
should have found expression in a work which will in all
probability outlive many such fashions.

> ' Vitium tanto conspectius in se
> Crimen habet quanto major qui peccat habetur.'

We have often thought that a curiously interesting book
might be written on the posthumous fortune of poets. In the
case of prose writers, the verdict of the age which immediately
succeeds them is, as a rule, final. Their reputation is subject
to few fluctuations. Once crowned, they are seldom deposed;
once deposed, they are never reinstated. Time and accident
may affect their popularity, but the estimate which has been
formed by competent critics of their intrinsic worth remains
unmodified. How different has been the fate of poets! Take
Chaucer. In 1500 his popularity was at its height. During
the latter part of the sixteenth century it began to decline.
From that date till the end of William III.'s reign—in spite of
the influence which he undoubtedly exercised over Spenser, and
in spite of the respectful allusions to him in Sydney, Putten-
ham, Drayton, and Milton—his fame had become rather a
tradition than a reality. In the following age the good-
natured tolerance of Dryden was succeeded by the contempt of
Addison and the supercilious patronage of Pope. Between
1700 and 1782 nothing seemed more probable than that the
writings of the first of England's narrative poets would live
only in the memory of antiquarians. In little more than half a
century afterwards we find him placed, with Shakspeare and
Milton, on the highest pinnacle of poetic renown. Not less
remarkable have been the vicissitudes through which the fame
of Dante has passed. During the fourteenth century he was
regarded with superstitious reverence. Indeed, his reputation
was so jealously guarded, that a pretext was found to bring a
contemporary,

contemporary, who had presumed to parody his verses, to the stake. In the fifteenth and sixteenth centuries his fame greatly declined, and he sank to a position similar to that assigned to Ennius by the Augustan critics. During the seventeenth century there were distinguished critics even among his own countrymen, who not only placed him below Petrarch and Ariosto, but even disputed his title to be called a Classic. The sentence passed on him by Voltaire and Bettinelli is well known; and though he never, it is true, wanted apologists, there can be no doubt that Voltaire and Bettinelli represented the general opinion of the eighteenth century. Then came the reaction. From the time of Monti his influence on the literatures of Italy and England has been prodigious. Every decade has added to his fame, and that fame, gigantic though it is, is even now increasing.

Still more singular has been the fortune of the fathers of our drama. It was their lot to obtain from contemporaries what most poets obtain only from a later age, their just deserts. They were, as a rule, neither over-praised nor under-valued. Nothing can be more discriminating than the judgment passed on the dramas of Marlowe, Greene, and Lyly by the generation which witnessed their appearance. But, strange to say, the justice which was so readily done them by contemporaries was destined to be persistently withheld from them by after ages. It is not surprising that their fame should have been eclipsed by the fame of their successors; it is still less surprising that the revolution which dethroned their successors should have buried them in oblivion. But that their merits should have been so tardily recognized when, at the beginning of the present century, the tide turned in favour of our earlier dramatists, is inexplicable. Yet so it was. Jonson, Beaumont, Fletcher, Ford, Massinger, Shirley, had found enthusiastic editors when the dramas of the masters of Shakspeare were still uncollected. It was not till 1826 that Marlowe received the honour of being edited. Greene and Peele had to wait still longer. Six of Lyly's plays had, it is true, been reprinted in 1632, but half the present century had passed before a full and adequate edition of his dramas appeared. It was natural that when the reaction came, it should come with a force proportioned to the persistency with which it had been delayed. It has come with a force which may well astound all who are not acquainted with the characteristics of reactions in criticism. The number of essays and monographs, the object of which is to heap indiscriminate eulogy on these poets, passes calculation. One writer gravely compares Marlowe with Æschylus. Another writer,
and

and we regret to say that that writer is Mr. Symonds, speaks of Greene as a Titan. We have seen Lyly placed on a level with Molière, and the author of the 'Arraignment of Paris' exalted above the author of the 'Aminta.' Indeed the length to which this fulsome and ridiculous rhodomontade is now being carried is positively sickening. We are not, as we hope to show, in any way insensible to the merits of the poets to whom we have alluded. We are quite willing to go as far as Lamb and Hazlitt in eulogistic criticism, and in our opinion Lamb and Hazlitt went quite far enough. Every one who knows anything of the world knows that the most mischievous form which detraction can assume is exaggerated praise. Calumny may be repelled or lived down, but the man who is overpraised is continually forced to give the lie to his own reputation. And what is true of men who live in the world, is true also of men who live only in the memory of the world. The reputation of Richardson has suffered more from the extravagant panegyrics of Rousseau and Diderot, than from the ridicule of Fielding and the sneers of Sterne. The noblest passage in the drama of the Restoration is, in consequence of Johnson's absurd encomium, now rarely quoted except to be laughed at; and we quite agree with Blair, that Parnell would stand much higher in popular estimation had his merits not been so preposterously over-rated by Hume. In the interests, therefore, of these poets themselves, as well as in the interests of criticism, we protest against this fashion of exaggerated panegyric. It cannot fail to operate most perniciously on public taste, and it cannot fail in the end to defeat its own object.

The history of the Early English Drama may be divided with some precision into three epochs. The first extends from about the end of the eleventh century to about the middle of the fifteenth. This is the period of the mysteries and miracles, and its distinctive feature is the predominance of the sacred over the secular element; in other words, the absorption of the miracle, which was of literary origin, in the mystery, which was of liturgical origin. Between the middle of Henry VI.'s reign and the beginning of Elizabeth's, this rude drama assumed other forms. In the moralities, which now superseded the earlier plays, it approached more nearly to the character of a work of art. It became less simple and less uncouth. Under the disguise of allegory it began to exhibit increasing ingenuity in the structure of the fable. Under the disguise of abstractions, its *dramatis personæ* grew more and more true to nature and life. Nor was this all. It brought itself into more immediate contact with contemporary society and with contemporary history. If its spirit was
didactic,

didactic, it was not didactic in the sense in which the mysteries
and miracles are didactic. It was no longer subservient to
settled dogma. It emancipated itself from Mediævalism, it
allied itself with an awakening world. Nowhere, indeed, is
the history of the revolution which transformed the England of
Mediævalism into the England of the Renaissance, written more
legibly than in these plays. In such moralities, for example, as
' The Castle of Perseverance ' and ' The Interlude of Youth,' the
old faith still reigns dominant and unimpaired. In ' Lusty
Juventus ' and in ' New Custom,' the doctrines of the Reforma-
tion have triumphed over the doctrines of Catholicism; and in
the ' Conflict of Conscience,' the struggle between the old faith
and the new is depicted with an energy which is almost tragic
in its intensity. In ' The Nature of the Four Elements ' and in
' Wit and Science,' we have, on the other hand, remarkable
illustrations of the emancipation of the morality from reli-
gion. In these pieces the theological element entirely disap-
pears. Their object, so far at least as it is didactic, is simply
to awaken a love of science. They reflect the influence of the
Renaissance on that side in which the Renaissance was most
hostile to the body from whom in the first instance the drama
had emanated, and to whom for so many generations the drama
had been loyal. But if the influence of the new science is
perceptible in these plays, the influence of the new learning is
not less perceptible in such a morality as ' The Triall of
Pleasure.' Here we find that indiscriminate use of materials
derived from the classics and material derived from the Bible,
that intermixture of paganism and Christianity which was one
of the essential characteristics of the literature of the Renaissance.

The next step in the history of the morality is the substitution of fictitious or historical personages for abstract figures, and
the subordination of the allegorical to the dramatic element,—
an innovation so simple and so obvious, that it is not a little
surprising that it should have been accomplished so gradually
and delayed so long. It was effected at last by the ' Interludes '
of Heywood, and by the ' Chronicle Play ' of Bale. These Interludes became in their turn the model on which Still, some years
later, framed his ' Gammer Gurton's Needle,' and thus the transition to regular comedy was complete. Not less clearly is the
transition from the morality to the history marked by Bale's
' Kyng John.' In this play we find the abstractions of the
morality resolving themselves into historical characters. Thus
Sedition becomes Stephen Langton ; Private Wealth, Cardinal
Pandulph ; Usurped Power, Innocent III. It is only a step from
' Kyng John ' to the ' Famous Victories of Henry V.,' and
' The

'The Troublesome Raigne of King John,' in which abstract characters and didactic allegory entirely disappear, and an historical play, in the proper sense of the term, presents itself.

So closes what may be called the second period in the history of our national drama. And it is perhaps worth pausing to notice how curiously that history repeated itself, not indeed chronologically, but in all its essential features in almost every country in Europe. In Italy we have the *Misterio* and the *Miracolo*, the *Favola Morale* and the *Farsa*, a species of drama which answers in one of the forms it assumed to our Interludes, and side by side with these we find the ' History Play.' In France we have the *Mystère* and the *Miracle*, and then we have the *Moralité*, and we see the morality and the mystery passing on the one hand into the farce and the *Sotie*, and on the other hand into the ' History.' That mysteries and miracles were among the earliest forms which the drama assumed in Spain, and that these were succeeded by ' moralities,' cannot reasonably be doubted, though no specimens have, we believe, survived. Certainly the *Entremises* correspond exactly to the Interlude.

But though during this second period the transition from the mystery and the morality, from comedy to history, was techni- cally effected, the circumstance is less important than it would at first sight appear to be. It is indeed natural to suppose, as it commonly is supposed, that the drama of Marlowe and Shak- speare was but a further development of the drama we have been discussing. Such, however, was not the case. We will not go so far as to say that there are no traces in the Romantic drama of the influence of these earlier and ruder plays, for there are many, particularly in comedy, occasionally even in Tragedy.* But this we will venture to affirm, that had these early plays never existed the Romantic drama would have sprung up independently ; would have presented the same features ; would have run the same course. In other words, we believe that the moralities and interludes stand in the same relation to the Romantic drama as the Fabulæ Atellanæ and the Etruscan Mimes stood to the drama of Ancient Rome. Roman tragedy owed nothing to the Atellan Fables. Roman comedy owed nothing to the Etruscan Mimes. Both were exotics. The one sprang immediately from Greek tragedy, the other sprang immediately from Greek comedy. By no process of evolution

---

* The Good Angel and the Evil Angel in Marlowe's 'Faustus,' and the part played by the Devil in Greene's ' Friar Bacon and Friar Bungay,' the abstractions of the Dumb Show in ' The Warning for Fair Women,' in ' Mucedorus,' in ' Soliman and Perseda,' and in Yarington's ' Two Tragedies in One,' are cases in point. The Shakspearian Clown, undoubtedly a lineal descendant of the Satan of the Mysteries and of the Vice of the Moralities, is a more important illustration.

could

could the drama as it existed in Rome between B.C. 363 and
B.C. 240 have developed into the drama which obtained in
Rome between B.C. 240 and B.C. 50. By no process of evolution
could the drama of Bale and Heywood have developed into
the drama of Marlowe and Peele. To what source then is the
Romantic drama to be traced? We answer unhesitatingly, to
the Italian drama of the Renaissance.

The popularly accepted theory that Elizabethan tragedy and
comedy flowed directly from the older plays, that tragedy is
simply the miracle and morality modified by the study of
Seneca and the Italian tragedians, and that comedy is simply
the interlude modified by the comedy of Ancient Rome and
Renaissant Italy, is in our opinion a theory which could be
held by no one who had studied with attention the drama of the
Italian Renaissance. As this is a question of some importance,
and as our opinion may perhaps appear somewhat paradoxical,
we will state our reasons for dissenting from the popular theory.

If what is technically known as the Romantic drama be compared with the older plays, we shall find that it is distinguished
from them by three striking peculiarities. In the first place it
is divided into five acts, or, if not so divided, is so constructed
as to admit of such a division—in other words, it possesses a
regular plot regularly unravelling itself on definite principles.
In the second place, imagination and fancy enter largely into its
composition; and in the third place, it is, in its diction, studious
of the beauties of poetry and rhetoric. Now these characteristics
are, as we need scarcely say, the characteristics of the Classical
drama. And yet if we compare a page or two of any of our
Romantic dramatists with a page or two of a Roman dramatist,
we should at once feel that the older poet could have had no
direct influence on the later. If, for example, we place 'Gorboduc,' a play closely modelled on Seneca, side by side with
'Tamburlaine,' or 'Edward II.,' we shall have no difficulty in
understanding how wide is the interval which separated Roman
tragedy from ours. Again, take comedy as formulated by Lyly
and Greene and perfected by Shakspeare. It is clearly no mere
development of the interlude. It as clearly owes little or
nothing to Plautus and Terence.

We turn to Italy, and all is explained. We there find a
drama presenting all the chief features of our Romantic drama
—that classicism which is not the classicism of antiquity, that
realism which is not the realism of unilluminated life. There,
we contend, are to be found the models on which Marlowe and
his contemporaries consciously or unconsciously worked. It
was there that the Romantic drama was virtually promulgated.
There,

There, not in England, was accomplished the revolution which transformed the tragedy of Seneca into the tragedy of Marlowe, and the comedy of Plautus and Terence into the comedy of Lyly and Greene.

It is remarkable that from the very first there was a marked tendency on the part of Italian playwrights to romantic innovation. This is seen even in the Latin Plays. Among the earliest of them we find comedy blended with tragedy, a constant attempt to escape from the thraldom of the unities, and an ostentatious realism substituted for the ideality of the classical stage. Their plots, moreover, are frequently drawn from contemporary history, though in this, as we need scarcely say, they found precedents in the Tragedy of the ancients. Thus Verardo's ' Historia Bætica,' written about 1490, is founded on the expulsion of the Moors from Granada, and is in everything but in diction and structure our Chronicle Play. The words of the Prologue are so remarkable that we will quote them :—

> ' Requirat autem nullus hic Comediæ,   ?
> Leges ut observentur aut Tragœdiæ,
> Agenda nempe est Historia, non fabula.'

In Mussato's 'Eccerinis' and in Laudivio's ' De Captivitate Ducis Jacobi,' we have striking illustrations of this romanticizing tendency. The first dramatizes the career of Eccelino de Romano, and the second dramatizes the fall of Jacopo Piccinino. Both, therefore, are studies from real life, both embody in artistic form familiar incidents. In both the language is the language of Seneca, but the spirit and feeling are the spirit and feeling of contemporaries. And what is apparent in the Latin plays becomes, as we might naturally expect, far more apparent in the vernacular. It is not too much to say that by the middle of the sixteenth century the vernacular classical drama had undergone so many modifications, that it presents almost all the characteristics of the Romance. To deal first with style. We find plays written in tercets, in the ottava rima, and in *versi sdruccioli;* we find rhyme and blank verse mingled ; we find blank verse variously modified, monotonously stately, loosely colloquial, broken and spasmodic, fluent and diffuse ; we find prose substituted for verse. In the comedies of Angelo Beolco and Andrea Calmo, we even find the *dramatis personæ* speaking in the dialects of the cities to which they belong. We see, in fine, a constant attempt to cast off the shackles of rigid classicism. Another important link between the Italian drama and the Romantic, is the fact, that it rejected rhyme in favour of blank verse on precisely the same ground. Blank verse, it was

said,

said, being less artificial than rhyme, is better adapted to express
the passions and to appeal to the passions. 'Rima denota,'
says Antonio Cavallerino, in the Discourse prefixed to his
'Rosamunda,' 'pensamento e premeditatione, e che le cose
ch' appaiono pensate e premeditate, estinto il verisimile, estin-
guono insieme la compassione e lo spavento che nascono ne
gli spettatori da quella credenza, c' hanno che le cose accaschino
allora in scena.' In tone and structure these dramas adhere, it
must be admitted, much more closely to Roman models. And
yet even in these respects important differences are discernible.
As tragedies they have more colour, they have more warmth,
they have more life than their prototypes. If their plots are similar in their evolutions, they are as a rule richer in incident. If, in
imitation of a vicious original, the action too often stagnates in
arid dialectics, it is as often animated by nature and passion.

Of the obligations of the Romantic stage to the Italian with
regard to machinery, there can be no question. Every one
knows with what effect the Elizabethan playwrights employed
the echo; how they delighted in the play within the play;
how common it was for a Chorus to explain the action; how
frequently the ghosts of great men appeared in the capacity of
Prologue; how elaborate the character and how imposing the
use made of the dumb show; how important the part played
by apparitions, how wide the space filled with physical horrors.
All this was undoubtedly learned from Italy. The dumb show
had, it is true, been popular in England long before any influence from Italy can be traced on our drama, and the shades of
the dead had figured, as we need scarcely say, among the
dramatis personæ of the ancient stage. But it was reserved for
the Italians to discover their full effect as dramatic auxiliaries,
and it was as elaborated by Italian ingenuity that they make
their appearance in our Romantic drama.*

But the influence of the Italian drama on ours is seen most
conspicuously in the fact, that it furnished examples of almost
every species of dramatic composition which obtained among us
during the latter half of the sixteenth century. From the Latin

---

* See particularly the 'Discorso della Poesia rappresentativa,' by Angelo
Ingegneri, printed at Ferrara in 1598. As Ingegneri's remarks about the proper
way of representing ghosts are well worth attention, and as the work is not very
accessible, we will quote a short passage : 'L' ombra doverebbe esser tutta coperta,
più che vestita, di zendale over altra cosa simile, pur di color nero, e non mostrar
nè volto, nè mani, nè piedi e sembrare in sommo una cosa iuforme. . . . E quanto
al parlare, aver una voce alta e rimbombante, ma ruvida ed aspra e in conchiusioue
orribile e non naturale, servando quasi sempre un istesso tuono.' For the ghost
in action, see Speroni's 'Canace,' Decio's ' Acripanda,' Corraro's 'Procne,' and
Manfredi's 'Semiramide.'

plays of Mussato and Laudivio sprang the Latin plays of Legge,
Gager, Alabaster, and others. From the Italian imitators of
Seneca sprang Sackville and Norton's 'Gorboduc,' Gascoign's
'Jocasta,' and Hughes's 'Misfortunes of Arthur.' Indeed Gascoign's 'Jocasta' is, as Mr. Symonds has for the first_time
pointed out, a free version of Dolce's 'Giocasta.' From such
plays as Antonio da Pistoia's 'Pamphila,' Rucellai's 'Ros-
munda' and Groto's 'Hadriana,' sprang 'Tancred and Gismund,' and the numerous plays of which 'Tancred and
Gismund' is the type. From the tragedies of Cinthio and
Mondella sprang the two famous tragedies of Kyd and the
tragedy of 'Soliman and Perseda.' From the 'Calandra' of
Bernardo Divizio, from Machiavelli, and from the 'Cassaria'
and the 'Suppositi' of Ariosto, Lyly learned to clothe comedy
in prose. On the 'Boscareccie Favole' was modelled Peele's
'Arraignment of Paris,' and on the 'Farse,' Greene's 'Orlando
Furioso' and Peele's 'Old Wives' Tale.' Luca Contile
and Epicuro had invented, or rather revived, Tragi-Comedy.
Domestic Tragedy dates from the 'Il Soldato' of Angelo
Leonico (1550), and what are known in our drama as Histories—plays, that is to say, founded on recent historical incidents—had precedents in Mondella's 'Isifile,' and in Fuligni's
'Bragadino,' the first of which appeared in 1582, and the second
in 1589.

Nor are these resemblances between the Italian and the
English drama likely to have been mere coincidences. Of the
intimate connection between England and Italy during the early
and latter parts of Elizabeth's reign, and of the popularity of
Italian literature in England during these years, there can be no
question. Its study had been facilitated by grammars and
dictionaries, by guides to its beauties, and by guides to its pro-
nunciation. As early as 1578, an Italian Company was acting
in London. No man's education was held to be complete till
he had visited the cities which were to an Englishman of that
age what Athens and Corinth were to the contemporaries of
Horace, and till he had, in the phrase of the time, returned home
'Italianated.' That Gascoign, Greene, Munday, Lodge, and Nash
travelled in Italy is certain, and it is very likely that, if more
was known of the lives of Peele and Marlowe, we should find that
they too had performed the customary pilgrimage. However
that may be, they were undoubtedly well-read in the literature
of Italy. It could hardly, indeed, have been otherwise. The
taste was universal. At the Universities and in London an
Italian quotation was the symbol of the cultured. The classics
of modern Italy were as reverently studied as the classics of
antiquity.

antiquity. Those who could not read the originals, contented themselves with translations, and the number of translations which appeared· between the accession of Elizabeth and the accession of James I. was immense. Ascham complains that Petrarch was preferred to Moses, and that the 'Decameron' was more highly estimated than the Bible. That the English playwrights were in the habit of indulging in wholesale plagiarism from their brethren in Italy, is proved by Gosson, who tells us that the Italian Comedies 'were ransacked to furnish matter for the London theatres.' It would not perhaps be too much to say that in the case of nearly two-thirds of the Elizabethan Dramas, where they are not Comedies or Histories, the plots may be traced to Italian sources. But it was only natural that the power which had revolutionized our literature should revolutionize our drama. Since the publication of Tottel's 'Miscellanies' in 1557, English genius had been as completely under the spell of Italy, as seventeen centuries before Roman genius had been under the spell of Greece, and as a century afterwards French genius was under the spell of Rome. We have not the smallest doubt that Marlowe and Greene regarded Bale and Heywood as Actius and Terence regarded the authors of the Atellan Farces, and as Racine and Molière regarded Rutebeuf and Bodel.

We must, however, guard carefully against attaching undue importance to the influence of Italy. It was an influence the significance of which is purely historical. All it effected was to furnish the artists of our stage with models, it operated on form, and it operated on composition, but it extended no further. Once formulated, our drama pursued an independent course. It booame, in the phrase uf its greatest representative, 'the very age and body of the time, his form and pressure'—in style and diction of unparalleled richness and variety, in subject-matter co-extensive with human experience and human imagination. To no eye, indeed, but to the eye of the critical historian would there seem to be anything in common between those living panoramas of nature and manners the Romances of Elizabethan England, and the stately declamations which won the plaudits of the Academia de' Rozzi and the Academia degl' Intronati.

With the accession of Elizabeth commences what may be called the third period in the history of our stage. More than a quarter of a century had still to elapse before Marlowe and his coadjutors revolutionized dramatic art. Of the plays produced between 1558 and 1586 probably not more than one-third have escaped the ravages of time. But there is no reason to suppose, that those which are lost differed in any

important

important respect from those that remain, and enough remain to enable us to form a clear conception of the state of dramatic literature during these years. Regarded comprehensively, that literature is represented by three distinct schools. On the one side stand a body of playwrights who adhere to the traditions of the vernacular drama, and who reproduce in forms more or less modified the moralities and interludes. On the other side stands a large and influential body who treated these rude medleys with disdain, and owned allegiance only to classical masters. Between these two schools stands a third, which united the characteristics—or, to speak more accurately, many of the characteristics—of both. And from the appearance of 'Gorboduc' to the appearance of 'Tamburlaine' these three schools co-existed, each pursuing an independent course. We have thus the extraordinary anomaly of a drama, crude, rudimentary, semi-barbarous, flourishing contemporaneously with a drama as perfect in form as the most finished pieces of the Roman and Italian stage. It would at first sight appear almost incredible that such plays as 'Horestes,' 'Tom Tiler and his Wife,' and 'Like to Like,' should have succeeded such plays as 'Ralph Roister Doister' and 'Gorboduc,' and that an age which had witnessed 'Tancred and Gismund' could tolerate twelve years afterwards the 'History of Sir Clyomon and Sir Clamydes.' But this anomaly is easily explained. The inequality between these plays corresponds with the inequality of the audiences to which they were addressed. Till the last decade of Elizabeth's reign there were two distinct spheres of dramatic activity. At the Inns of Court, at the Court itself, at the Universities, at the public schools, nothing was tolerated which did not bear the stamp of classicism. It was for such audiences that Sackville and Norton parodied Seneca, Udall Plautus, and Spenser Ariosto and Machiavelli ;* that Gascoign adapted Dolce's 'Giocasta' and Ariosto's 'Gli Suppositi ;' that Hatton and his coadjutors wrote 'Tancred and Gismund,' Thomas Hughes 'The Misfortunes of Arthur,' and Lyly 'Campaspe' and 'Endymion.' Of a very different order were the spectators who gathered in the inn-yards of the Bell Savage and the Red Bull, and in the playhouses on the Bankside and in Shoreditch, and of a very different order were the performances in which they delighted. No class is so conservative as

---

* These Comedies of Spenser's have unfortunately perished, but their character and our loss are sufficiently indicated in one of Gabriel Harvey's Letters to him : 'I am voyd of all judgement if your nine Comedies whereunto, in imitation of Herodotus you give the names of the Nine Muses, come not nearer Ariosto's Comedies eyther for the fineness of plausible eloqution or the rareness of poetical invention than that Elvish Queene doth to his Orlando Furioso.'

the vulgar. The spell of tradition is potent with them long after it has lost its efficacy with others. What found most favour in their eyes was what had found favour in the eyes of their forefathers. They clung fondly to all that was peculiar to the old stage, to the old buffoonery, to the old didacticism, to the old half-farcical, half-serious allegorizing, to the old realism, to the vice, to the abstractions, to the gingling doggerel, to the cumbersome quatrains. In one respect, indeed, these plays differed from those of the former generation. The material out of which preceding playwrights constructed their plots lay within a comparatively narrow compass. The cry now was for novelty. The history and fiction of all ages and all countries was ransacked for matter to weave into dramas. ' I may boldly say it, because I have seen it,' says Gosson, 'that " The Palace of Pleasure," " The Golden Ass," " The Æthiopian History," " Amadis of France," and " The Round Table," comedies in Latin, French, Italian and Spanish have been thoroughly raked to furnish the playhouses in London.' Nothing came amiss to these indefatigable caterers for popular amusement. They drew indiscriminately on pagan mythology and on medieval legend, on incidents in history and on incidents in private life. Of these dramas, probably few found their way into print, and scarcely any have survived. But the loss, if we may trust the opinion of competent judges, and if those which remain are samples of those which have disappeared, is assuredly no matter for regret. The contempt with which they were regarded by polite critics is shown and justified by what Whetstone, Gosson, and Sydney have written concerning them. They appear, indeed, to have been little better than wild and improbable medleys, as coarse and bungling in construction as they were vulgar and cumbersome in style.

But of these early schools the most interesting from an historical point of view is the third. It was the aim of the representatives of this school to create a drama out of elements furnished by each of the other schools. They followed popular models in blending tragedy with comedy, in cultivating a spirit of homely fidelity to nature and life, and in embodying dramatic dialogue in rhymed verse. But classical models guided them in the evolution of their plots, in their anxiety to avoid gross violation of the unities, and in their attempt at dignity and propriety of diction. As samples of the plays of this school we have Richard Edwards' 'Damon and Pytheas,' and George Whetstone's ' Promos and Cassandra.' The last, which is preceded by a singularly interesting preface, explaining the principle on which it was written, has more than

one

one title to attention. It was the work on which the greatest of poets founded his ' Measure for Measure,' and it was the first formal vindication of some of the leading principles of Romanticism. Whetstone regarded the medleys in vogue with the vulgar with just disdain, but he saw clearly that too strict an adherence to the canons of classicism was in every way undesirable. He chose, therefore, a middle course. He avoided the extremes of both, but he adopted something from each.

Such was the condition of the English drama when that illustrious company of playwrights who immediately preceded Shakspeare entered on their career.

We remember to have read in some medieval writer a story to this effect. A traveller on enchanted ground found himself in the course of his wanderings in a wild and spacious valley. Around him were all the indications of fertility, rich even to rankness. The trees rose dense and high ; heavy parasites hung in festoons from their trunks and branches ; thick mantling shrubs matted the glades at their feet. Wherever his eye rested, it rested on what appeared to be exuberant vegetation. But the spectacle proved on a nearer view to be delusive. He soon perceived that what he beheld was the semblance of fecundity, not the reality. The trees and the parasites which clung to them were without bloom and without vitality ; the underwood which appeared to be flourishing so vigorously beneath, was arid and dwarfed. Scarcely a flower he saw was worth the culling. Scarcely any of the fruits that had ripened were worth the gathering. Suddenly as by magic the scene changed. Every tree, every shrub, burst into luxuriant life. The leaves and the grass were of the hue of emeralds; the ground was ablaze with flowers. All was perfume, all was colour. He stood dazzled and intoxicated amid a wilderness of sweets—a teeming paradise of tropical splendour. Very similar to the phenomenon witnessed by the traveller of the fable is the phenomenon presented to the student of English poetry at the period on which we are now entering. From the beginning of the sixteenth century there had been no lack of literary activity. With what assiduity the drama had been cultivated we have already seen ; with what assiduity other branches of poetry were cultivated will be apparent to any one who will glance at a catalogue of the writers who flourished during these years. And yet, voluminous as this literature is, how little has it contributed to the sum of our intellectual wealth ! how frigid, how lifeless, does it appear when placed in contrast with the literature which immediately succeeded it ! The revolution which gave us the ' Faery Queen ' for the ' Mirror for Magistrates,' the lyrics of of Greene and Lodge for the lyrics of Gascoign and Turberville, the sonnets of Daniel for the sonnets of Watson, the Eclogues of Spenser for the Eclogues of Googe, 'Tamburlaine' for 'Gorboduc,' and 'Friar Bacon and Friar Bungay' for 'Ralph Roister Doister' and 'Misogonus,' seems like the work of enchantment. It was in truth the work of an age rich beyond precedent in all that appeals to the emotions and to the imagination, operating on men peculiarly susceptible of such influences and possessed of rare powers of original genius.

The golden era of Elizabethan literature may be said to date its commencement from the seven years which lie between 1579 and 1587,—in other words, with the first characteristic poems of Spenser and the first characteristic plays of Marlowe, with the publication of 'Euphues' and with the composition of the 'Arcadia.' Never, perhaps, has there existed an age so fertile in all that inspires and all that nourishes poetic energy as that which opens the third decade of Elizabeth's reign. It was commensurate with a great crisis in European history, and with a great crisis in European thought. The discomfiture of the partisans of Mary of Scotland, the execution of Mary herself, and the destruction of the Armada in the following year, had paralyzed that mighty coalition which had long been the terror of Protestant Europe. The effect of the events of 1588 on the world of Marlowe and his contemporaries was indeed similar to the effects of the Persian victories on the world of Phrynicus and Æschylus. In both cases what was at stake was the very existence of national life. In both cases were arrayed in mortal oppugnancy the Oromasdes and the Arimenes of social and intellectual progress. In both cases the moral effects of the triumph achieved were in proportion to the magnitude of the issues involved. Joy, pride, and hope possessed all hearts. The pulse of the whole nation was quickened. The minds of men became preternaturally active, and every faculty of the mind preternaturally alert. Nor was this all. The forces at work in that mighty revolution which transformed the Europe of Medievalism into the Europe of the Renaissance were everywhere fermenting. It was the fortune of England to pass simultaneously through two of the greatest crises in the life of states, and the excitement of the most momentous of epochs in her spiritual history was coincident with the excitement of the most momentous of epochs in her political history. The energy thus stimulated operated on materials richer and more various than perhaps any other age could have afforded. Philosophy, having cast off the shackles of scholasticism, had entered on the splendid inheritance which had descended to it
from

from antiquity. Astronomy was unravelling the secrets of the skies, and Natural Science the secrets of the land and sea. Heroes, second to none in the annals of endurance and adventure, were exploring every corner of the habitable globe, and coming home to record experiences as marvellous as those which Ulysses poured into the ears of Alcinous and Arete. The Muse of History had awakened with Grafton and Stowe, and Hall and Holinshed; (and the Muse of Romantic Fiction with Malory and with Malory's numberless successors.) The Translators of the Bible had unlocked the lore of the East. Scholars were revelling among the treasures of that noble language which, in the fine expression of Gibbon, 'gives a soul to the objects of sense and a body to the abstractions of philosophy,' and which has during more than twenty centuries been to the world of mind what the sun is to the physical world. The study of Roman literature had been rendered more fruitful by the precedence now given to the Classics of the Republic and Early Empire over the writers of the Later Ages. 'The youth everywhere,' says Strype, 'addicted themselves to the reading of the best authors for pure Roman style, laying aside their old barbarous writers and schoolmen.' All that had been contributed to the general stock of intellectual wealth by modern Italy was becoming more and more familiar to Englishmen, and scarcely anything of note appeared either in France or Spain which was not sooner or later pressed into the service of English genius.

But there were other sources of inspiration, other stores on which the writers of that age could draw. The world in which they moved was in itself rich in all the materials which poetry most cherishes. In the first place there had, for many centuries, been gradually accumulating an immense mass of local traditions. Every county, nay, every hundred and every city in England, had its heroes and its annals. We have only to open works like Warner's 'Albion's England,' and Drayton's 'Polyolbion,' to see that there was scarcely a mountain, a river, a forest, which did not teem with the mingled traditions of history and fable. The mythology, out of which Livy constructed the early chronicles of Latium, was in truth not more dramatic and picturesque than that which lived on the lips of Elizabethan England. Much of this lore had been embodied in rude ballads—some of it had found its way into the Metrical Romances, and more recently into 'The Mirror for Magistrates,' but it owed its popularity to oral transmission. With this heroic mythology was blended a mythology which had its origin in superstition. To the England of the sixteenth century the
                                                              unseen

unseen world was as real as the world of the senses. Its voices were everywhere audible, its ministers were everywhere present. What reason has with us coldly resolved into symbolism was with them simple fact. The substantial existence of the Prince of Darkness and the Powers of Hell, of the Bad Angel who is man's enemy, and of the Good Angel who is his friend, was no more questioned by an ordinary Englishman of that day than the existence of the human beings round him. In his belief the communion between the world of the living and the world beyond the tomb had never been interrupted. What Endor witnessed, was in his opinion, what half the churchyards in England had witnessed. The angels, which were of old beheld passing and repassing between earth and heaven, passed, it was believed, and repassed still on their gracious errands. 'It may,' says one of the most popular writers of those times, 'be proved from many places of the Scripture that all Christian men have not only one angell, but manie whom God employeth to their service.' Nor was it from the Bible only that the supernatural creed of that age was derived. The awful forms with which the sublime and gloomy imagination of the Goths had peopled the tempest and the mist ; the elves, fays, and faeries, and all that 'bright infantry,' who, in the graceful mythology of the Celts, hold high revel—

'On hill, in dale, forest or mead,
By paved fountain or by rushy brook,
Or on the beachèd margin of the sea'

—the Demons of the fire 'who wander in the region near the moon,' the Demons of the air 'who hover round the earth,' Mandrakes and Incubi, Hellwaines and Firedrakes, these were to the people of that age as real as the objects which met their view in daily life, and to doubt their existence was, says Grose, held to be little less than Atheism.*

If again we turn to the social life of those times we find ourselves in a world equally picturesque, and equally calculated to awaken poetry. In the country dwelt a race as blithe and simple as that which peopled the Sicily of Theocritus or the Delos of the Homeric Hymn. The English peasantry had, even when groaning under the yoke of a martial and despotic aristocracy, been distinguished by their lightheartedness and love of social merriment. They were now in the first intoxication of newly-found freedom. They were now, for the first time in their history, settled and prosperous. If the happiness of a class is to

---

* Whoever would understand how completely even the most enlightened minds of that age were under the dominion of these superstitions would do well to turn to Henry More's 'Antidote against Atheism.'

be estimated by its wealth and political importance, it would be
absurd to point to the sixteenth century as the Golden Age of
rural England.   But those whose criterion is not that of the
Political Economist, will, we think, agree with Goldsmith, that
this was in truth the Saturnian era of English country life.   No
fictitious Arcadia has half the charm of the world described to
us by Stubbes and Stowe.   It was a world in which existence
appears to have been a perpetual feast.   Every house had its
virginal, its spinnet, and its lute.   Each season of the year had
its festivals.   At Christmas every farmstead and country mansion,
garnished with holly and evergreens, and bright with the blazing
yule, rang with tumultuous mirth.   Songs and dances, possets
and loving-cups, ushered in, amid pealing bells, the New Year;
and the New Year's revels were often protracted till it was time
to wreathe the wassail-bowls and marshal the pageants of
Twelfth-Night.   Then came the feasts of Candlemas and
Easter, which terminated the festivities of Easter and opened
the festivities of Spring.   On May-day all England held carni-
val.   Long before it was light the youth of both sexes were in
the woods gathering flowers and weaving nosegays.   By sun-
rise there was not a porch or door without its chaplet, and,
while the dew was still sparkling on the grass, the may-pole had
been dressed, 'twentie or fortie yoke of oxen, everie oxe having
a sweet posie of flowers tied to the tip of his horns drawing it
solemnly home.'   On its arrival at the appointed place it was
set up.   The ground round it was strewn with hawthorn sprays
and green boughs.   Summer-hall booths and arbours were
erected on each side of it.   Processions from the neighbouring
hamlets, headed by milkmaids leading a cow festooned with
flowers and with its horns gilt, were a common feature in these
picturesque festivities.   Nor was it the younger people only
who kept festival.   'In the month of May,' says Stowe—we
cannot resist quoting this exquisitely beautiful passage—'namely
on May Day in the morning every man, except impediment,
would walk into the sweet meddowes and green woods, there to
rejoice their spirits with the beauty and savour of sweet flowers
and with the harmonie of birdes praysing God in their kinde.'
It would have required very little sagacity to foretell that a
world such as this was destined to bear rich fruit in poetry.

And yet at no period in its history did our poetry pass through
so perilous a crisis.   For some time it seemed not unlikely that
the Renaissance would cast the same spell on English genius as
it had cast on the genius of Italy and France.   Its effect there
had been to kindle an enthusiasm for the works of the ancients,
so intense and absorbing that it amounted to fanaticism; a
                                                    fanaticism

fanaticism against which all the forces which commonly direct, and all the causes which commonly inspire intellectual and artistic activity, were powerless to contend. No art escaped the infection, but poetry suffered most. A wretched affectation of classical sentiment, of classical imagery, of classical diction, pervaded it. To write tragedies in the style of Seneca, and comedies in the style of Plautus, to construct, out of materials furnished by Theocritus and Virgil, roccoco Arcadias, to parody Pindar and Simonides in dithyrambs, and Ovid and Claudian in tinsel idylls, became the employment of men, who, had they succeeded in casting off the fetters of this degrading servitude, might have attained no mean rank among poets. Thus poetry became completely divorced from nature and life, losing all sincerity, losing all originality. An exception, indeed, must be made in favour of the Romantic School, but even the Romantic School passed under the yoke. That our poetry narrowly escaped the same fate cannot, we think, be doubted. When we remember the superstitious reverence with which the writings of antiquity were regarded, the ardour with which the study of these writings was pursued, the ridiculous extent to which the affectation of learning was carried in the pulpit, in Parliament, and even in the taverns and playhouses, the classicism and pseudo-classicism predominant everywhere in academic and aristocratic circles,* the enormous popularity of the literature of Italy, the influence exercised by that literature, the contempt for Romanticism at the Court and at the Universities, the constant endeavours on the part of both to dethrone it, and, above all, the culture and learning which distinguished the Romancists themselves; when, too, we remember how deeply tainted much of our poetry actually was; take for example the comedies of Lyly, the tragedies of Lady Pembroke, Brandon, and Daniel, the lyrics of Greene and Constable, the poems of Chapman, the masques and dramas of Jonson; we cannot but feel how real, how imminent was the danger. Fortunately, however, the instinctive energy of genius prevailed; fortunately the England of Elizabeth was not the Italy of Leo; fortunately

---

* 'When the Queen paraded through a county town almost every pageant was a Pantheon. When she paid a visit at the house of any of her nobility, she was saluted by the Penates and conducted to her privy chamber by Mercury. Even the pastrycooks were expert mythologists. At dinner select transformations of Ovid's Metamorphoses were exhibited in confectionery, and the splendid iceing of an immense historic plum-cake was embossed with a delicious basso-relievo of the destruction of Troy. In the afternoon, when she condescended to walk in the garden, the lake was covered with Tritons and Nereids; the pages of the family were converted into wood nymphs, who peeped from every bower, and the footmen gambolled over the lawns in the figure of Satyrs.'—Warton, 'History of English Poetry,' vol. iv. page 323.

our

our poetry had its roots in a soil so rich that the parasites which
might, under less propitious conditions, have choked its growth
and exhausted its vitality, served only

> ' —to become
> Contingencies of pomp.'

And that that poetry should have found its chief expression
in the drama is not surprising. The age was, in itself, pre-
eminently an age of activity. It had no tendency to intro-
spective brooding; it troubled itself, as a rule, very little about
the ideal; it was no worshipper of Nature. Its central figure
was man in action; its distinguishing characteristic was its
sympathy with humanity. Thus human life, its failures, and its
triumphs; thus human kind, their passions and peculiarities,
became objects of paramount interest. Nor was this all.
London was already the centre of the social and intellectual life
of the kingdom, and was attracting each year from the provinces
and the Universities all who hoped to turn wit and genius to
account. The refuge of literary adventurers in our day is the
periodical and daily press. In those days there were no journals
and no periodicals, for there was no reading public. But among
the changes introduced by the dissolution of the old system was
the appearance and rapidly-increasing importance of a class,
which corresponded to that on which our popular press relies
for support. Since the accession of the Tudors, a great change
had passed over London. Peace and a settled government had
transformed the rude and martial nobility of the Plantagenets
into courtiers and men of mode. Their hotels swarmed with
dependents who would, a generation back, have found occupation in the camp; but who were now, like their masters,
devoted to gaiety and pleasure. Contemporary with this revolution in the upper sections of society, was the rise of a great
commercial aristocracy. Each decade found London more
prosperous, more luxurious, more thickly-peopled. By the
middle of Elizabeth's reign she presented all the features peculiar to great capitals and great seaports. A large industrial
population, branching out into all the infinite ramifications of
mercantile communities, mingled its multitudes with the crowd
of men of rank and fashion, who affected the neighbourhood of
the Court, and with the swarms of adventurers and sycophants
who hung loose on the town or subsisted on the charity of noble
houses. The Inns of Court, thronged with students often as
accomplished as they were idle and dissolute, had already
assumed that half-fashionable, half-literary, character, which for
upwards of two centuries continued to distinguish them. But
no

no quarter of London stirred with fuller life than that which was then known as the Bankside. It was here that the lawless and shifting population, which came in and passed out by the river, found its temporary home. In the taverns and lodging houses which crowded those teeming alleys, were huddled together men of all nations, of all grades, of all callings ; Huguenot refugees, awaiting the turn which would restore them to their country ; Switzers and Germans who, induced partly by curiosity and partly by the restlessness which a life of adventure engenders, flocked over every year from the Low Countries ; half-Anglicized Italians and half-Italianated Englishmen ; Flibustiers from the Spanish Main, and broken squatters from the Portuguese settlements ; soldiers of fortune, who had fought and plundered under half the leaders in Europe ; Desperadoes, who had survived the perils of unknown oceans and lands where no white man had ever before penetrated ; seamen from the crews of Hawkins and Drake, and Cavendish and Frobisher. And among this motley rabble were to be found men in whose veins ran the blood of the noblest families in England—Strangways and Carews, Tremaynes and Throgmortons, Cobhams and Killigrews.

Such was the London of Elizabeth. It was natural that the cry of these people should be for amusement. Too intelligent to be satisfied with the stupid and brutal pastimes then in vogue with the vulgar, and too restless and illiterate to find pleasure in books, it was equally natural that they should look to the stage to supply their want. And the stage responded to the call.

In 1574, Elizabeth granted to James Burbage, and four other players, the right of exhibiting dramatic performances within the precincts of the City. This was strongly opposed both by the Puritans and by the Common Council. A memorial was addressed to the Queen. A counter-memorial, on the part of the players followed. At last a compromise was effected. Burbage and his company, quitting the strict limits of the City, established themselves in Black Friars. The construction of a regular theatre was begun. The Puritans were furious ; the burgesses of Black Friars petitioned ; but Burbage triumphed, and London had its first play-house. From this moment dates the commencement of the modern stage. The temporary platforms which had been erected, as occasion required, in inn-yards, in the yard, for example, of the Bull, in Bishopsgate Street, and the Belle Savage, on Ludgate Hill, now gave place to permanent theatres. The erection of Burbage's Black Friars theatre in 1576 was followed in the same year by the erection of ' The Theatre ' and ' The Curtain ' in Shoreditch. Each decade added to the number, and in the latter years of Elizabeth's reign London
could

could boast of at least eleven of these edifices. What had before scarcely risen to the dignity of a distinct vocation now became a thriving and lucrative profession. The strolling companies who, under the real or pretended protection of noble houses, roamed the country, now flocked, certain of employment, to the metropolis. Indeed, the demand for those who could produce, and for those who could act, plays was such that the supply, though abundant, almost to miraculousness, could scarcely keep pace with it.

In an incredibly short space of time the semi-scholastic, semi-barbarous drama of preceding playwrights was transformed into that wonderful drama in which, as in a mirror, the world of those times saw itself reflected, which, in its infinite flexibility, adapted itself to every taste, to every understanding ; which, in its all-absorbing, all-assimilating activity disdained nothing as too mean, excluded nothing as too exalted, and which, in its maturest manifestations, is among the marvels of human skill and human genius. In little more than twelve years from its first appearance that drama had not only superseded every other form of popular entertainment, but had cast into the shade every other school of contemporary poetry. It had disputed the pre-eminence of the classical playwrights by turning against them their own weapons. Declamation, as ornate and stately; dialogue, as brilliant with antithesis and as rich with the embellishments of scholarship and culture as had ever won the applause of Elizabeth and Leicester, was now heard in every playhouse from Shoreditch to Southwark. It had rivalled the poetry of Spenser in gorgeousness of diction and in teeming fertility of imagination and fancy. No narrative poetry since Chaucer's could compare with it in vividness of description and portraiture. In pastoral poetry, nothing equal to its pictures of country life and country scenery had appeared since the Sicilian Idylls. It had pressed into its service the graces of the lyric and the sonnet. It had enriched itself with all that Sydney and his circle had borrowed from Petrarch and Sannazaro, and with all that Lyly and his disciples had derived from Spain. And it had transformed what it had borrowed. It had extended the dominion of art. It had revealed new capacities in our language and new music in our verse. To the fathers of this drama belongs the glory of having moulded that noble metre which, even in their hands, rivalled the iambic trimeter of Greece, but which was in the hands of its next inheritor to become the most omnipotent instrument of expression known to art.

We will now, as far as our space will permit, pass in review the chief of those remarkable men who were the fathers of our

Romantic

Romantic drama ; and who, whatever may be their inferiority in point of genius, are certainly entitled to the honour of having been the masters of Shakspeare—Thomas Kyd, Robert Greene, George Peele, Christopher Marlowe, and the unknown author of 'Arden of Faversham.' In the lives and characters of these men where particulars have survived, there is so much in common, that it is as easy to describe them collectively as separately. They were all men peculiarly typical of the New Age. They were all sprung from the lower and middle classes ; they were all born in the provinces ; they had all gone up from the provinces to the Universities ; and from the Universities, with the object of seeking a livelihood as authors by profession, to London. They were all thorough men of the world. They had all had ample experience of either fortune. They were all of them dis-tinguished, even in those wild times, by the ostentatious disso-luteness of their lives, and they all of them came prematurely to mournful and shameful ends. Not less striking was the similarity between them in point of genius and culture. They were all scholars. Peele translated one of the ' Iphigenias '; Mar-lowe paraphrased the poem of the Pseudo-Musæus, and has left versions of Ovid's 'Amores,' and the first book of the ' Pharsalia.' The Sapphics and Elegiacs of Greene cannot indeed be commended for their purity or elegance ; but they are a sufficient indication of his mastery over the Latin language, and what is true of the Sapphics and Elegiacs of Greene is true also of the hexameters of Kyd and Marlowe. Of their familiarity with the. literatures of modern Europe, there is scarcely a page in their writings which does not afford abun-dant proofs. Indeed, in mere learning, and in their fondness for displaying that learning, they bear some resemblance to the poets of Alexandria and Augustan Rome ; but though they owed much to culture, they owed more to nature. They were all of them pre-eminently poets. They had all, in the phrase of Juvenal, bitten the laurel. In all of them the faculties which enable men to excel as painters of life and manners were subordi-nate to the faculties which impress lyric poetry with grace and fancy, and narrative poetry with picturesqueness and dignity. If we except Kyd and the author of ' Arden of Faversham,' they have all left plays which stand higher as poems than as dramas ; and two of them have left poems which are superior to the best of their plays. Marlowe's ' Hero and Leander ' is intrinsically a finer work than either his ' Faustus ' or his ' Edward II.'; and his ' Passionate Shepherd ' is, in our opinion, worth a dozen ' Tamburlaines.' Of Greene's plays, charming as many of them are, the most that can be said is that they scarcely entitled him

to

to a place among dramatists of the second order. Of Greene's lyrics, the least that can be said is that they are among the best of their kind in our literature. Regarded as dramas, Peele's plays are almost worthless; as ornate and musical declamations they are often admirable.

Of these poets, the youngest in years but the first in importance was Christopher Marlowe. Born in Feb. 1563–4, the son of a shoemaker at Canterbury, he received the rudiments of his education at the King's School in that city. He subsequently matriculated at Benet College, Cambridge, taking his degree as Bachelor of Arts in 1583, and his degree of Master of Arts four years later. Of his career at Cambridge, and of his movements between 1583 and 1587, nothing is known. It is probable that by the end of 1587 he had settled in London, having already distinguished himself by the production of 'Tamburlaine.' The rest of his life is a deplorable record of misfortune, debauchery, and folly, suddenly and fearfully terminated before he had completed his thirtieth year, by a violent death in a tavern-brawl at Deptford.

When Dryden observed of Shakspeare that he found not, but created first the stage, he said what was certainly not true of Shakspeare, but what would, with some modification, be true of Marlowe. To no single man does our drama owe more than to this ill-starred genius. It was he who determined the form which Tragedy and History were permanently to assume. It was he who first clothed both in that noble and splendid garb which was ever afterwards to distinguish them. It was he who gave the death-blow to the old rhymed plays on the one hand, and to the frigid and cumbersome unrhymed classical plays on the other. In his 'Doctor Faustus,' and in his 'Jew of Malta,' it would not be too much to say that he formulated English romantic tragedy. He cast in clay what Shakspeare recast in marble. Indeed, Marlowe was to Shakspeare in tragedy precisely what Boiardo and Berni were to Ariosto in narrative. It is certain that without the 'Orlando Innamorato' we should never have had the 'Orlando Furioso.' It is more than probable that without the tragedies of Marlowe we should never have had, in the form at least in which they now stand, the tragedies of Shakspeare. Of the History in the proper sense of the title Marlowe was the creator. In his 'Edward I.' Peel·had, it is true, made some advance on the old Chronicles.* But the difference between Peele's 'Edward I.' and Marlowe's 'Ed-

---

* Though the date of the publication of Peele's 'Edward I.' is subsequent to that of Marlowe's 'Edward II.,' we have little doubt that, in point of composition, it preceded Marlowe's play.

ward II.' is the difference between a work of art and mere botch-work. Peele's play is little better than a series of disconnected scenes loosely tagged together; superior indeed in style, but in no way superior in structure to the 'Famous Victories of Henry V.,' and to the 'Troublesome reign of King John.' In 'Edward II.' Marlowe laid down, and laid down for all time, the true principles of dramatic composition as applied to history. He showed how, by a judicious process of selection and condensation, of modification and suppression, the crowded annals of many years could in effect be presented within the compass of a single play. He studied perspective and symmetry. He brought out in clear relief the central figure and the central action, grouping round each in carefully graduated subordination the accessory characters and the accessory incidents. Chronology and tradition, when they interfered either with the harmony of his work or with dramatic effect, he never scrupled to ignore or alter, rightly discriminating between the laws imposed on the historian and the laws imposed on the dramatist. He was the first of English playwrights to discern, that in dramatic composition the relative importance of events is determined not by the space which they fill in history, but by the manner in which they impress the imagination and bear on the catastrophe. Nor are these Marlowe's only titles to the most distinguished place among the fathers of English tragedy. He was not only the first of our dramatists who, possessing a bold and vivid imagination, possessed also the faculty of adequately embodying its conceptions, but the first who, powerfully moved by strong emotion, succeeded in awakening strong emotion in others. In the hands of his predecessors tragedy had been powerless to reach the heart. As a rule, it had maintained the same dead-level of frigid and nerveless declamation. In his hands it resumed its ancient sway over the passions; it unlocked the sources of terror and pity. To compare Marlowe with the Attic dramatists would be in the highest degree absurd; and yet we must go back to the Attic dramatists to find anything equal to the concluding scenes of 'Dr. Faustus' and 'Edward II.'

The appearance of 'Tamburlaine' has been compared to the appearance of 'Hernani.' Its professed object was to revolutionize the drama. The war which Victor Hugo declared against classicism Marlowe declared against

'The jiggling verses of rhyming mother wits
And such conceits as clownage keeps in pay.'

The most remarkable of his innovations was the substitution of blank verse for rhyme and prose. It would not, of course, be true to say that Marlowe was the first of our poets to employ blank verse in dramatic composition. It had been employed by Sackville and Norton in 'Gorboduc;' by Gascoign, in 'Jocasta;' by Lyly, in his 'Woman in the Moon;' by Hughes, in his 'Misfortunes of Arthur;' and by the authors of other plays which in all probability preceded 'Tamburlaine.' But these plays had been confined exclusively to private audiences, and had not been designed for the popular stage. Nor must we confound the blank verse of Marlowe with the blank verse of these dramas. In them it differed only from the heroic couplet in wanting rhyme. It had no variety, no incatenation, no harmony; in the contemptuous phrase of Nash, it was a drumming decasyllabon, and a drumming decasyllabon there seemed every probability of it continuing to remain. It is remarkable that since its first introduction into our language by Surrey, though it had passed through the hands of poets whose other compositions show that they possessed no common mastery over metrical expression, its structure had never altered. The genius of Marlowe transformed it into the noblest and most flexible of English metres. If we examine the mechanism of his verse, we shall see that it differed from that of his predecessors in the resolution of the iambic into tribrachs and dactyls; in the frequent substitution of trochees and pyrrhics for monosyllables, in the interspersion of Alexandrines, in the shifting of the pauses, in the use of hemistichs, in the interlinking of verse with verse. It was therefore no mere modification, no mere improvement on the earlier forms of blank verse: it was a new creation.

The effect of Marlowe's innovation was at once apparent. First went the old rhymed stanzas. We doubt whether it would be possible to find a single play written in stanzas subsequent to 1587. Next went the prose histories. Then commenced the gradual disappearance of rhymed couplets. Thus plays which previous to 1587 were written in rhyme, we find after 1587 interpolated with blank verse. Such is the case with the 'Three Ladies of London;' such is the case with 'Selimus;' such is the case with the recast of 'Tancred and Gismund.' Before 1587 Peele habitually employed rhyme; after 1587 he discarded it entirely. Greene, who, if we interpret rightly an ambiguous passage in his Epistle prefixed to 'Perimedes,' regarded Marlowe's innovation with strong disfavour, almost immediately adopted it. In all his extant dramas blank verse is employed. By 1593 it was firmly established.

How profoundly the genius of Marlowe impressed his contemporaries is evident not only from the frequent allusions to his

his writings, but from the imitations, close even to servility, of his characters and his style, which abound in our dramatic literature between 1587 and 1600. Sometimes we have whole plays which are mere parodies of his; such would be Green's 'Alphonsus' and Peele's 'Battle of Alcazar;' such also would be the anonymous play, 'Lust's Dominion.' His Barabas and Tamburlaine took the same hold on the popular imagination as the Conrads and Laras and Harolds and Manfreds of a later age, appearing and reappearing, variously modified in numerous forms. Tamburlaine became the prototype of the stage hero. Barabas became the prototype of the stage villain. To enumerate the characters modelled on these creations of Marlowe would be to transcribe the leading *dramatis personæ* of at least two-thirds of the heroic dramas in vogue during the latter years of the sixteenth century. Indeed the influence—and we are speaking now not of the general, but of the particular influence—exercised by Marlowe over the works of his brother-poets would, if traced in detail, be found to be far more extensive than is generally supposed. To go no further than Shakspeare. 'Richard the Second' is undoubtedly modelled on 'Edward II.;' the character of Richard is the character of Edward slightly modified. In the Second and Third Parts of 'Henry VI.,' if Shakspeare did not actually work in co-operation with Marlowe, he set himself to imitate with servile fidelity Marlowe's method and Marlowe's style. Aaron in 'Titus Andronicus' is Barabas in the 'Jew of Malta;' so in some degree is Shylock; so in a considerable degree is 'Richard III.' In the nurse who attends on Dido we have a sort of first sketch of the Nurse in 'Romeo and Juliet.' From the 'Jew of Malta' Shakspeare derived many hints for the 'Merchant of Venice.' From the concluding scene of 'Dr. Faustus' he borrowed, or appears to have borrowed, one of the finest touches in 'Macbeth.' *

From an historical point of view it would therefore be scarcely possible to over-estimate the importance of Marlowe's services. Regarded as an initiator, he ranks with Æschylus. But criticism must distinguish between merit which is relative and merit which is intrinsic. It may sound paradoxical to say of the father of our Romantic drama, of the master of Shakspeare, that his genius was in essence the very reverse of dramatic, nay, that the temper of his genius was such as to absolutely disqualify from excelling as a dramatist. And yet

---

* In both tragedies a storm is raging without, while the deeds of horror are proceeding in ghastly silence within. Cf. the last scene of 'Faustus,' edit. 1616, and 'Macbeth,' Act II., s. 3. It is of course possible that the scene may have been interpolated by another and later hand and borrowed from 'Macbeth.'

such

such is the case.   In Marlowe we have the extraordinary
anomaly of a man in whom the instincts of the artist and the
temper of the poet met in mere oppugnancy.   Induced partly
perhaps by the exigencies of his position, partly no doubt
influenced by the age in which it was his chance to live, the
materials on which he worked he elected to cast in a dramatic
mould.   Nature had endowed him with a singular sense of
fitness and harmony, with an appreciation of form Greek-like
in its delicacy and subtilty.   This is conspicuous in all he has
left us, in his too scanty lyric poetry, in his too scanty narrative
poetry.   When, therefore, he applied himself to dramatic composition, the same instinct directed him unerringly to the true
principles on which a drama should be constructed.   It caused
him to turn with disgust from the rude and chaotic style of the
popular stage ; it preserved him, on the other hand, from the
pedantry and affectation of the classical school.   In a word,
what propriety of expression, what nice skill in the technique
of his art, could accomplish, that Marlowe achieved, and the
achievement has made his name memorable for ever in the
history of the English drama.

But the moment we turn from Marlowe as an artist to
Marlowe as a critic of life, we feel how immeasurable is the
distance which separates him, we do not say from Shakspeare,
but from many of the least distinguished of his brother playwrights.   His genius and temper have been admirably described
by Drayton :

> 'Next Marlowe, bathèd in the Thespian springs,
> Had in him those brave translunary things
> That the first poets had ; his raptures were
> All ayre and fire which made his verses clear,
> For that fine madness still he did retain
> Which rightly should possess a poet's brain.'

It was in this translunary sphere that he found his characters ;
it was under the inspiration of this fine madness that he
delineated them.   Of air and fire, not of flesh and blood, are
the beings who people his world composed.   Regarded as
counterparts of mankind, as studies of humanity, they are mere
absurdities.   They are neither true to life nor consistent with
themselves.   Where they live, they live by virtue of the intensity
with which they embody abstract conceptions.   They are
delineations, not of human beings, but of superhuman passions.

The truth is, that in the constitution of Marlowe's genius—
and we are using the word in its widest sense—there were serious
deficiencies.   In the first place, he had no humour ; in the second
place, he had little in common with his kind, and with the
ordinary

ordinary men of ordinary life, nothing; a defect which seems to us as detrimental to a dramatist as colour-blindness would be to a painter. In the faculty, again, of minute and accurate observation—a faculty which is with most dramatists an instinct—he appears to have been almost wholly lacking. Nothing is so rare in Marlowe as one of these touches, which show that the poet had, as Wordsworth expresses it, 'his eye on his object.' His dramas teem with blunders and improprieties such as no writer who had observed mankind even with common attention could possibly have committed; and in the vagueness and conventionality of the epithets which are in almost all cases applied by him to natural objects, we have conclusive evidence of the same defective vision.

The words in which Sallust describes Catiline will apply with singular propriety to Marlowe: 'Vastus animus semper incredibilia, semper immoderata, nimis alta cupiebat.' This is in truth Marlowe's distinguishing characteristic. It is one of the sources of his greatness as a poet; it is the main source of his weakness as a dramatist. It was to him what the less exalted egotism of a less exalted nature was to Byron. If we except Edward II., all his leading characters resolve themselves into mere incarnations of this passion. In Tamburlaine and Guise it is the illimitable lust for dominion. In Barabas it is the illimitable lust for wealth. In Faustus it is the insanity of sensual and intellectual aspiration. As impersonations of mankind neither Tamburlaine nor Guise, neither Barabas nor Faustus, will bear examination for a moment. Of Marlowe's minor characters there is not one which impresses itself with any distinctness on the memory. Indeed they have scarcely more individuality than the 'fortisque Gyan, fortisque Cloanthus' of the 'Æneid,' or those heroes in the 'Iliad' who are mentioned only to swell the number of the slain. Who ever realized Mycetas or Techelles, or Usumcasane or Mathias, or Ferneze or Ithamore, or Lodowick? What distinguishes Amyras from Celebinus? Or Jacomo from Barnardine? Or Valdes from Cornelius? Or Calymath from Martin del Bosco? Take again his women. Where they are not mere puppets, as is the case with Zenocrate, Abigail, Bellamira, and Catharine, they are preposterously untrue to nature, as is the case with Olympia, Isabella, and Dido. In one play, and in one play only, has Marlowe displayed a power of characterization eminently dramatic. In 'Edward II.,' Gaveston, Mortimer, and the King himself are as admirably drawn as they are admirably contrasted. The sculptural clearness with which the figure of Mortimer, cold, stern, remorseless, stands out from the crowded canvas;

canvas; the light but firm touches which place the King's young favourite, the joyous, reckless, pleasure-loving Gaveston, vividly before us ; the power and subtilty with which the quickly alternating emotions in the breast of Edward, from his first conflict with opposition to his last appalling agony, are depicted —all these combine to place this drama on a higher level than any of Marlowe's other plays. 'Edward II.' is said to have been the poet's last work. If it was so, it shows that, as his life advanced, his genius was widening and mellowing, and it increases our regret for the accident which cut short his career. But that we lost in Marlowe a possible rival of Shakspeare is an opinion in which we by no means concur. It is true that though the two poets were born within a few weeks of each other, Marlowe was the master and Shakspeare the disciple. It is true also that the best work produced by Shakspeare at twenty-nine —to judge at least from what he gave to the world—was greatly inferior to the best work of Marlowe. But this proves little more than that the powers of Shakspeare were, up to a certain point, slow in developing, and that is almost always the case with men whose genius is of an objective cast. What we fail to see in Marlowe is any indication of power in reserve. Comparatively scanty as his work is, he is constantly repeating himself, and in the few noble and impressive scenes on which his fame as a dramatist mainly rests, we discern what is perhaps the most unpromising of all symptoms in the work of a young writer, excessive elaboration. That 'Edward II.' is a considerable advance on his former plays, that it is marked throughout by greater sobriety, and that it exhibits a wider range of sympathy and insight than he has elsewhere displayed, is indisputable. But this is all, and this is not much. In a dramatic poet of the first order we look for qualities which are as conspicuously absent in Marlowe's last and maturest play as they are in the plays which preceded it.

We are not, then, inclined to assign to Marlowe that high position among dramatists which it has of late years been the fashion, and in our opinion the absurd fashion, to claim for him. But as a poet he seems to us to deserve all the praise which his admirers give him. The words rapture and inspiration, which are, when applied to most poetry, little more than figurative expressions, have, when applied to his poetry, a strict propriety. Never before had passion so intense, had an imagination so vivid and aspiring, had fancy so rich and graceful, co-existed in equal measure and in equal harmony.

The energy of Marlowe's genius was twofold. On the one side he is a transcendental enthusiast ; on the other side he is a Pagan Hedonist.

Hedonist. On the one side he reflects the intense spiritual activity, the preternatural exaltation, not merely of the emotions, but of the imagination and the intellect which were among the most striking effects of the Renaissance in England. On the other side he reflects not less faithfully the peculiarities of that great movement as it affected Academic Italy. The ardour of his passion for the ideal, and the intensity with which he has expressed that passion, are what impress us most in his dramas. In his poems, on the other hand, the predominating element is pure sensuousness. It is the poetry not of desire, but of fruition. No poem in our language is more classical, in the sense, at least, in which Politian and Sannazaro would have understood the term, and assuredly no poem in our language is more sensuously lovely, than ' Hero and Leander.' It reminds us in some respects of the best episodes in the ' Metamorphoses,' and it reminds us still more frequently of Keats's narratives, not, indeed, of ' Isabella ' or of the ' Eve of Saint Agnes,' but indirectly of ' Endymion,' and directly of ' Lamia.'

But of all Marlowe's gifts the most remarkable, perhaps, was his gift of expression. It may be said of him, with literal truth, that he ' voluntary moved harmonious numbers.' Of the music of his verse it is superfluous to speak. On this point we are inclined to go almost as far as Mr. Swinburne. If the melodies of Shakspeare and Milton are fuller and more complex; if the music of the poets, who have during the present century revealed new capacities in our language, has a subtler fascination, no clearer, no nobler, no more melodious note than the note of Marlowe vibrates in our poetry. His diction too, when at its best, as we see it, for example, in ' Hero and Leander,' in the lyric ' Come and live with Me,' and in such passages in his plays as Tamburlaine's speech to Zenocrate, as Faust's apostrophe to the shade of Helen, as Edward's last speeches to Leicester, as Guise's soliloquy, as Baldwin's speech to Spenser, seems to us to approach as nearly to the style of the Greek masterpieces as anything to be found in English. It is the perfection of that diction which is at once natural and poetical, at once simple and dignified.*

Next in importance to Marlowe comes Robert Greene. Of all the writers who between 1584 and 1592 followed literature

---

* We gladly take this opportunity of directing attention to an edition of Marlowe's complete works, recently edited by Mr. A. H. Bullen. It appears to us to contain an excellent recension of the text, and reflects great credit on the Editor, who is, we understand, engaged on a new Edition of the principal pre-Shakspearian Dramatists. If the volumes which follow are as carefully edited as this, the first instalment of the series is, Mr. Bullen will be conferring a great boon on all who are interested in the Early English Drama.

as

as a profession, Greene was the most fertile and the most popular. 'In a day and a night,' says his friend Nash, 'would he have yarked up a pamphlet as well as in seven years, and glad was that printer that might be so blest as to pay him dear for the very dregs of his wit.' He distinguished himself as a poet, as a novelist, as a social satirist, and as a playwright. And to Greene, both as an individual and as an author, a peculiar interest attaches itself. In the first place no man of that age is so well known to us, for he has himself, in some of the most remarkable confessions which have ever been given to the world, laid bare the innermost secrets of his life. In the second place he is, of all our writers, the writer who illustrates most clearly the exact nature of the influence exercised by the Renaissance on English genius; and in the third place, there is about many of his writings a singular charm and grace. He was born at Norwich, probably about 1560. In due time he proceeded to Cambridge, taking his Bachelor's degree as a member of St. John's College in 1578, and his Master's five years later as a member of Clare Hall. At Cambridge he appears to have been equally distinguished by his profligacy and his abilities. Between 1578 and 1583 he travelled on the Continent, visiting Italy, France, Spain, Germany, Poland, and Denmark. He returned, he tells us, an adept in all the villainies under the heavens, a glutton, a libertine, and a drunkard. But he returned, it is certain, with other and more honourable attainments—with rich stores of observation and experience, with a genius polished and enlarged by communion with the classics of Rome and Florence, and with a mind profoundly impressed by the loveliness and splendour of the lands which Nature loves. He commenced his literary career about 1583, with a prose novel, 'Mamillia,' which was three years afterwards succeeded by a Second Part; and as this is dated from his study in Clare Hall, it is probable that he resided at Cambridge between the period of his return from the Continent and his taking his Master's degree. By 1586 he had apparently settled in London. The story of Greene's life, from this period to his death, has been so often told, that it is quite unnecessary to tell it again here. We will only say that for our own part we are strongly inclined to suspect that his debaucheries have been very much exaggerated. That he was a man of loose principles and loose morals, and that he was reckless and improvident, is evidently no more than truth; but that he was what his enemies have asserted, and what he himself, under the influence of religious reaction, morbidly aggravated by remorse, represented himself to have been

—a

—a prodigy of turpitude—seems to us utterly incompatible with facts. Greene's life was and must have been a life of incessant literary activity. It is almost certain that many of his writings have perished, and yet enough remains of his poetry and prose to fill eleven goodly volumes, and enough survives of his dramatic composition to fill two volumes more. And all this was the work of about eleven years. Now making every allowance for rapid and facile workmanship, is it within the bounds of possibility that a man sunk so low in sensuality and dissoluteness as Greene is said to have been, could in that time have produced so much, and so much, we may add, that was good? Again, four years before his death, he was incorporated at Oxford, a certain proof that well known as his name must have been—for he was then in the zenith of his fame, scandal had not been busy with it there. Nor is this all. His patrons and patronesses were to be found among the most virtuous and honourable persons then living. It is not, indeed, likely that the Riches and Arundels, the Talbots and Stanleys, troubled themselves very much about the private life of a needy man of letters; but it is very certain that had Greene's excesses been as notorious as we are told they were, he would never have dared to address the Lady Fitzwaters or the Lady Mary Talbot as he addresses them on the dedications of ' Arbasto' and ' Philomela,' and he would scarcely have ventured to subscribe himself in a dedication to a man in the position of Thomas Barnaby ' your dutiful and adopted son.' But nothing is so conclusive as his writings. Not only are they absolutely free from any taint of impiety or impurity, but they were in almost all cases produced with the express object of making vice odious and virtue attractive, and in this laudable endeavour he was prompted by the noblest of motives. He was certainly no hypocrite, for the most malignant of his enemies could not have borne more hardly on his weaknesses than he has himself. He was not impelled by the love of gain, for though morality was popular in the fiction of that day, there is abundant evidence to show that immorality was much more popular. It is, moreover, due to Greene to say that the chief testimony against him is derived from his own confessions, and that, if these confessions afford evidence of his delinquencies, they afford not less certain evidence of the presence of a disease which caused him to magnify those delinquencies tenfold. Nothing can, we think, be clearer than that the mind of this unhappy man was, like that of Bunyan, distempered by religious hypochondria. In every page of his autobiographical pamphlets we are reminded of ' Grace Abounding.' He tells us, for example, how on one occasion he

he had an inward motion in Saint Andrew's Church at Norwich ;
how he was satisfied that he deserved no redemption, how a voice
within him told him that he would, unless he speedily repented,
be wiped out of the Book of Life ; how he cried out in the
anguish of his soul, Lord have mercy upon me, and give me
grace, but how he 'fell again, like a dog, to his vomit,' and
became in the judgment of the godly the child of perdition.
The world has long done Bunyan the justice he did not do
himself, and has rightly discriminated between facts as they
were and facts as his morbid fancy painted them. How necessary it is to make allowance for sensibilities similarly diseased
in the case of Greene will be evident from this. He has over
and over again reproached himself, and reproached himself
most bitterly, with prostituting his genius to unworthy purposes.
He speaks almost with agony of his amorous and wanton
pamphlets. He calls himself a second Ovid. 'But as I have,'
he says in the preface to his 'Mourning Garment,' 'heard with
the ears of my heart Jonas crying, Except thou repent—I have
resolved to turn my wanton works to effectual labours.' The
natural inference from this is that he had published works of a
grossly immoral character. But what is the truth ? There is
not, as we have already observed a single line in Greene's
writings which has the least tincture of impropriety. On the
contrary, scrupulous purity distinguishes everything which has
come from his pen. And that what he said had no reference to
works which are lost is absolutely certain. All he meant was
that the composition of love stories was an idle and frivolous
employment, unworthy of a man who aspired to teach, but this
became, when translated into the jargon of 'The Mourning
Garment' and 'The Repentance,' precisely what tipcat and
bell-ringing became when translated into the jargon of 'Grace
Abounding.' Now if Greene could, under the influence of religious hallucination, so totally and so absurdly misrepresent
himself as a writer, nothing can be more likely than that in his
confessions his character as a man has been equally distorted.
The truth is, that his proper place is, not as his biographers
would have us believe beside Boyse and Savage, but beside
Steele and Fielding, beside Goldsmith and Burns, in other
words, beside men who were rather morally weak than morally
depraved, whom we censure reluctantly and sincerely love, and
who, whatever may have been their infirmities, were sound in
the noble parts.

We have indulged ourselves in these remarks because we
frankly own that Greene is a great favourite with us. We
have read and re-read his poems, his novels, and his plays, and

                                                        at

at each perusal their pure and wholesome spirit, their liveliness, their freshness, their wealth of fancy and imagination, their humour, their tenderness, their many graces of style, have gained on us more and more. The best of his novels—and the best are undoubtedly 'Pandosto,' 'Philomela,' 'Never Too Late,' and 'The Groat's Worth of Wit,' though in some instances tainted with the vices of Euphuism—are in their way admirable. They strike, it is true, no deep chords, nor are they in reflection and analysis either subtle or profound, but they are transcripts from life, and they are full of beauty and pathos. Greene's favourite theme is the contrast between the purity and long-suffering of woman, and the follies and selfishness of man. In all the novels to which we have referred appears the same angelic figure ; in all of them the same meek, patient, blameless sufferer passes through the same cruel ordeal, and her tormentor is her husband. He is either insanely jealous, as is the case with Pandosto and Philippo in the two first novels, or unfaithful and dissolute, as is the case with Francesco and Roberto in the two last. In either case the life of the unhappy wife is one long martyrdom, and in depicting that martyrdom Greene shows a power and pathos not unworthy of him who painted the wrongs and virtues of Constance and Griselda. It is said that Greene drew, like Fielding, on his own experience, that he found his Bellarias, his Philomelas, his Isabellas, where Fielding found Amelia, in his own wife ; and that he found his Francescos, his Robertos, and his Phillippos where Fielding found Boothe, in himself. Of the autographical character of two at least of his novels, 'Never Too Late' and 'The Groat's Worth of Wit,' there can be no question.

Greene followed Sannazzaro in interspersing prose with poetry, and it is in his prose-writings that all his non-dramatic poetry is with one or two exceptions to be found. Mr. Symonds remarks that the lyrics of Greene have been under-rated. We quite agree with him. Greene's best lyrics are not indeed equal to the best lyrics of Lodge and Barnefield. In abandon and grace Rosalynde's madrigal is incomparably superior to Menaphon's song. In finish and felicity of expression Menaphon's picture of the maid with the 'dallying locks' must yield to Rosader's picture of Rosalynde, and charming as Greene's octosyllabics always are, they have not the charm of Barnefield's ' Nightingale's Lament.' But Greene's ordinary level is far above the ordinary level of both these poets. For one poem which we pause over in theirs, there are five which we pause over in his. He has, moreover, much more variety. What, for example, could

could be more exquisite, simple though it is even to homeliness, than Sephestia's song in 'Menaphon'? The tranquil beauty of the song beginning 'Sweet are the thoughts that savour of content,' in the 'Farewell to Folly,' and of Barmenissa's song in 'Penelope's Web,' fascinates at once and for ever. His fancy sketches are delicious. The picture of Diana and her bathing nymphs invaded by Cupid in the little poem entitled : 'Radagon in Dianam,' the picture of the journeying Palmer in 'Never Too Late,' of Phillis in the valley in 'Ciceronis Amor,' of—

> 'The God that hateth sleep,
> Clad in armour all of fire,
> Hand in hand with Queen Desire,'

in the Palmer's Ode are finished cameos of rare beauty. Not less charming are the love poems. Like all the erotic poetry of the Renaissance, they owe, it is true, more to art than to nature. Some of them are studies from the Italian, others from the French. Occasionally they appear to have derived their colouring from the Apocryphal books of the Bible. But the element predominating in them is classicism. Thus they appeal rather to the fancy than to the heart, rather to the senses than to the passions. And so graceful is their imagery, so rich is their colouring, so pure and musical is their diction, that they are never likely to appeal in vain.

To the composition of his plays Greene brought the same qualities, which are conspicuous in his novels and his poems, the same sympathetic insight into certain types of character and certain phases of life, the same fertility in inventing incident and detail, the same faculty of pictorial as distinguished from dramatic representation, the same refined pathos, the same mingled artificiality and simplicity, the same exuberant fancy, the same ornate and fluent eloquence of style. But he has brought little else. Such qualities never have sufficed, and never could suffice to produce dramas of the first order. In Greene's hands they have sufficed to produce dramas which, though not of the first order, are among the most delightful and fascinating productions of Elizabethan genius. But this praise applies, it must be admitted, only to three out of the six plays which have come down to us, and it would have been well for Greene's fame if the other three had perished. In that case his best work would not have been confounded, as it almost always is confounded with his worst. In that case his critics would not, like Mr. Symonds, have observed generally of his blank verse that it 'betrays the manner of the couplet,'

or

or generally of his style that it is cumbersome and pedantic. Indeed, the contrast between the plays of the first group,—' The History of Orlando Furioso,' 'Alphonsus King of Aragon,' and 'The Looking Glass for London and England,' which was written in conjunction with Lodge, and the plays of the second group,—' Friar Bacon and Friar Bungay,' ' James the Fourth of Scotland,' and ' The Pinner of Wakefield ' is in point of style so great that, if we had only internal evidence to guide us, we should be inclined to assign them to different writers. The two first were, in all probability, Greene's earliest attempts at dramatic composition in blank verse. They are in the style of Tamburlaine, and they reflect too faithfully the worst features of that work. But with all its fustian they have none of its music, with all its absurdities as a drama they have none of its beauties as a poem. The ' Looking Glass ' is a wild and silly medley, for which we suspect Lodge was mainly responsible. It is, therefore, as the author of the plays of the second group, and as the author of those plays only, that Greene deserves attention.

Of the importance of these plays in the history of our drama there can be no question. It is not too much to say that the author of ' Friar Bacon and Friar Bungay ' and of the ' Scottish History of James IV.' stands in the same relation to romantic comedy, as the author of ' Tamburlaine ' and ' Edward II.' stands to romantic tragedy. If, historically speaking, it is only a step from ' Edward II.' to ' Henry V.,' it is, historically speaking, only a step from ' Friar Bacon and Friar Bungay ' and ' James IV.' to the ' Two Gentlemen of Verona' and to ' As You Like It.' We have only to glance at the condition of comedy before it came into Greene's hands, to see how great was the revolution effected by him. On the popular stage it had scarcely cast off the shackles of the old barbarism. It still clung to the old stanzas; or if, as in the ' Knack to Know a Knave ' and in the ' Taming of a Shrew ' it employed blank verse, the blank verse was blank verse hardly distinguishable from prose. It still clung to the old buffoonery. It still remained unilluminated by romance or poetry. In the theatre of the classical school, on the other hand, it was a mere academic exercise, as it was with Lyly, or a mere copy from the Italian, as it had been with Gascoigne. We open Greene's comedies, and we are in the world of Shakspeare, we are with the sisters of Olivia and Imogen, with the brethren of Touchstone and Florizel, in the homes of Phebe and Perdita. We breathe the same atmosphere, we listen to the same language.

It was Greene who first brought comedy into contact with the
blithe

blithe bright life of Elizabethan England, into contact with poetry, into contact with romance. He took it out into the woods and the fields, and gave it all the charm of the idyll ; he filled it with incident and adventure, and gave it all the interest of the novel. A freshness as of the morning pervades these delightful medleys. Turn where we will—to the loves of Lacy and Margaret at merry Fressingfield, to the wizard friar and the marvels of his magic cell at Oxford, to the patriot Pinner and his boisterous triumphs, to Oberon with his faëries and antics revelling round him, to the waggeries of Slipper and Miles— everywhere we find the same light and happy touch, the same free joyous abandon. His serious scenes are often admirable. We really know nothing more touching than the reconciliation of James and Dorothea at the conclusion of 'James IV.,' and nothing more eloquent with the simple eloquence of the heart than Margaret's vindication of Lacy in 'Friar Bacon.' The scene again in the Second Act of 'James IV.,' where Eustace first meets Ida, would in our opinion alone suffice to place Greene in the front rank of Idyllic poets. Greene's plots are too loosely constructed, his characters too sketchy, his grasp and range too limited, to entitle him to a high place among dramatists, and yet as we read these medleys we cannot but feel how closely we are standing to the romantic comedies of Shak- speare. And the resemblance lies not merely generally in the fact, that the same unforced and genial energy is at work in both, and in the fact that both have, as it were, their roots in the same rich soil, but in particular resemblances. In Greene's women, in Margaret, for example, in 'Friar Bacon and Friar Bungay,' and in Ida and Dorothea in 'James IV.' we see in outline the women most characteristic of Shakspearian romantic comedy, while Slipper, Nano and Miles are undoubtedly the prototypes of the Shakspearian clown. Nor could any one who compares the versification and diction of Shakspeare's early romances with the versification and diction of Greene's medleys, fail to be struck with the remarkable similarity between them. It seems to us that Shakspeare owed at least as much to Greene as he owed to Marlowe. In the rhymed couplets and in the blank verse of his earlier comedies the influence of Greene is unmistakable, and we will even go so far as to say that the prose dialogue of Shakspeare—we are not of course speaking of his maturer plays—was modelled on the prose dialogue of Greene.

Third in the triumvirate with Marlowe and Greene stands George Peele. The merits of Peele have been greatly over-rated. They were ridiculously over-rated by his contemporaries. They have been inexplicably over-rated by modern critics. Gifford

classes

classes him with Marlowe. Dyce ranks him above Greene. Campbell, in an often-quoted passage, pronounces his David and Bethasabe to be the ' earliest fountain of pathos and harmony that can be traced in our dramatic literature,' and goes on to speak of the ' solid veracity ' and ' ideal beauty ' of his characters. The tradition that Milton borrowed the plot of 'Comus' from the ' Old Wives' Tale,' a tradition which appears to us absolutely without foundation, has, we suspect, greatly contributed to this factitious reputation. The truth is, that of Peele's six plays, there is not one which can be said to be meritorious as a drama or to have contributed any new elements to dramatic composition. Sir Clyomon and Sir Chlamydes is in the style of 'Damon and Pytheas,' and is, if possible, more insufferably dull. The 'Arraignment of Paris' is a mere pageant. Neither ' Edward the First ' nor the ' Battle of Alcazar ' contains a single effective scene, or a single well-known character, a single touch of genuine pathos, a single stroke of genuine humour. In the 'Old Wives' Tale' we have an attempt in the manner of Greene, but the difference between the medleys of Greene and the medley of Peele is the difference between an artfully-varied panorama and the anarchy of distempered dreams. From beginning to end it is a tissue of absurdities. Ulrici, indeed, discerns, or affects to discern, a profound allegory underlying these absurdities. We can only say that even with the clue which he has furnished we fail to see the allegory. Peele's best play is undoubtedly ' King David and Fair Bethsabe,' but it is best only in the sense of containing his finest writing. As a drama it is neither better nor worse than the others—that is to say, it is perfectly worthless.

Peele's sole merit lies in his style and in a certain fertility of fancy. His style cannot indeed be praised without reservation. It is too ornate; it is too diffuse; it is wholly lacking in nerve and energy, but it is flowing and harmonious. The heroic couplets in his ' Arraignment of Paris ' have a sweetness and fluency such as English versification had only occasionally attained before, and though his blank verse has the monotony necessarily characteristic of blank verse constructed on the model of the couplet, it is at times exquisitely musical. If that noble measure, which is to poetry what the organ is to music, owed its trumpet stop to Marlowe, it may, we think, with equal truth be said to owe its flute-stop to Peele. The opening scene of ' King David and Fair Bethsabe ' is in mere mellifluousness equal to anything which has been produced in blank verse since.

It is, we think, to be regretted that Peele did not follow the example of Guarini and Tasso. Had he applied himself to the
composition

composition of such works as the Aminta and the Pastor Fido, he would have excelled. In his drama may be discerned all the characteristics of those most pleasing poets,* the same delight in dallying with tender and graceful images, the same splendour of colouring, the same curious mixture of paganism and sentiment, the same instinctive selection of such scenes and objects in Nature as charm rather than impose; the same felicity in rhetorically portraying them; the same liquid harmony of verse; the same ornate elaboration of diction. Nor, on the negative side, is the resemblance less striking. Like them, Peele has no power over the passions, no rapidity of movement, nothing that stirs, nothing that elevates.

With the names of Marlowe, Greene, and Peele, are usually associated the names of Thomas Nash and of Thomas Lodge. Of Nash's dramas one only has survived, an absurd and tedious medley entitled: 'Summer's Last Will and Testament.' He is stated also to have been Marlowe's coadjutor in that wretched travesty of the fourth Æneid—'Dido, Queen of Carthage'— the most worthless portions of which may on internal evidence be with some confidence assigned to him. Nash's laurels were, it should be added, won on other fields. As a prose satirist he had neither equal nor second among his contemporaries. And what is true of Nash is true also of Lodge. Of all Lodge's multifarious writings, his contributions to the drama form the least valuable portion. He has written excellent prose pamphlets. His versions of Seneca and Josephus placed him beside North and Holland in the front rank of classical translators. He is the author of some of the most exquisitely graceful and musical lyrics to be found in our language. His 'Pastoral Poems,' and above all his 'Scilla's Metamorphosis,' though of a beauty too luscious and florid to please a severe taste, are among the best things of their kind. On his delightful prose romance 'Rosalynde, or Euphues Golden Legacy,' Shakspeare founded 'As You Like It,' and it is doing Lodge no more than justice to say that we still turn with pleasure from the drama to the novel. But his powers, versatile though they were, were not such as qualified him to excel as a dramatist. His only extant play—of his share in 'The Looking-Glass for London and England' we have already spoken—is 'The Wounds of Civil War.' It treats of the struggle between Marius and Sulla, and is based partly on Plutarch and partly on apocryphal matter, which is for aught we know Lodge's own invention. The plot is ill-constructed, the characters, though by no means without

* It is scarcely necessary to say that we are speaking of Tasso simply as the poet of the Aminta.

individuality,

individuality, are without interest, and the action, in spite of its studied variety, has all the effect of the most tiresome monotony.

In passing from this school of playwrights to Kyd, we pass to a dramatist whose proper place in the history of the Elizabethan stage it is extremely difficult to determine. Almost everything relating to Kyd rests on mere conjecture. We know neither the date of the composition of his plays, nor the date of their first appearance. Of the three extant dramas attributed to him, the authenticity of two is more than doubtful, and to complete our perplexity, the text of the only drama which is indisputably his has been largely interpolated by other hands. Indeed, all that is certainly known about him is that he was the author of a piece called the ' Spanish Tragedy,' that he translated, or, to speak more accurately, paraphrased Robert Garnier's 'Cornelia,' and that by the year 1598 he stood high among the tragic poets of his day. The two other plays, which have with more or less probability been ascribed to him, are ' Jeronimo,' which forms the first part of the ' Spanish Tragedy,' and a tragedy called ' Soliman and Perseda.' That ' Jeronimo ' is rightly attributed to him cannot, we think, be doubted by anyone who has compared it carefully with ' The Spanish Tragedy ' and 'Cornelia.' Ulrici's objections seem to us frivolous in the extreme. With regard to ' Solyman and Perseda ' we cannot speak with equal confidence. If it was written by Kyd it was probably his earliest work.

The popular notion about Kyd is that he was a sensational dramatist of the worst type; that he was the first to employ on our stage the ghastly and repulsive machinery of classical Italian melodrama; and that he expressed himself in a style which was worthy of Pistol. And this is true, but it is not the whole truth. Even admitting that the passages which Lamb calls the salt of ' The Spanish Tragedy ' are not from Kyd's hand, it is impossible to question the genius of the man who sketched in this and in the sister play the characters of Andrea, of Horatio, of Balthezar, of Lorenzo, of Jeronimo; who painted the parting scene between Andrea and Belimperia, and the scene in which Jeronimo and Isabella lament their murdered son. That his style is often absurdly stilted no one would deny, but this peculi.rity is rather its besetting fault than its distinguishing characteristic.

Kyd's services to English tragedy were, we think, more important than is commonly supposed. He stands midway between two great schools; between the Literary and Academic school on the one hand, and between the Domestic and Realistic

school

school on the other. Regarded superficially, he might perhaps be confounded with a mere copyist of Italian models. His diction is not unfrequently classical even to pedantry; he indulges largely in the arid and monotonous declamation peculiar to Italian tragedy; he delights in the exhibition of ' carnal, bloody, and unnatural acts.' And yet, with all this, the impression which his plays make on us is very different from the impression made on us by the Italian tragedies. Nor is it difficult to explain the reason. The canvas of Kyd is more crowded ; his touch is broader and bolder, his colour fuller and deeper ; his action is infinitely more diversified, animated, and rapid ; his characters are more human ; he has more passion, he has more pathos. If he aims too much at sensational effects, he is sometimes simple and natural. Again, his style when compared with that of the Italian school presents almost as many points of dissimilarity as it presents points of resemblance. It is, as a rule, freer and looser, of a coarser texture, of a more colloquial cast. We trace in it for the first time that curious mixture of homeliness and pomp, that rugged vigour, that sparseness of poetic ornament, that indifference to verbal harmony, which distinguish the style of the domestic plays. In a word, Kyd so modified classical tragedy, that he educed out of it a species of drama as distinct from that of Marlowe, -Greene, and Peele on the one hand, as it was distinct from that of Sackville, Gascoign, and Hughes on the other. It is this which constitutes his historical importance. It is this which connects him with that remarkable school of which we are about to speak, a school of which it would not indeed be true to say that he was the founder, but of which he was in many important respects the forerunner. We allude, of course, to the domestic dramatists.

In the theatre of Marlowe, Greene, and Peele the realistic element had, as we have seen, been subordinate to the poetic. It was as poets and scholars that they had approached the drama ; it was as poets and scholars that they constructed it. Hence they avoided with instinctive aversion all that was sordid, prosaic, and commonplace. Hence, in selecting their plots, they were careful to choose such subjects as recommended themselves by their dignity or grace. With equal solicitude had they employed all the resources of learning and rhetoric to elevate and embellish their style, and all the resources of imagination and fancy to cast the halo of poetry over life. The result was, that they had produced works which stand much higher as poems than as dramas—works which are not indeed without dramatic merit, and dramatic merit of a high order,

but

but which, where they reflect humanity, reflect it only in its heroic or poetic aspects. Wherever they had attempted, as they had sometimes done in comedy, to be strictly realistic they had signally failed.

With the writers of domestic tragedy it was exactly the reverse. With them the poetic element was not simply subordinate to the realistic, but almost entirely disappeared. Rejecting fiction they took their stand on naked fact. Rejecting transcendentalism, they prided themselves on their prosaic fidelity to prosaic truth. For the graces of expression they cared nothing.

'Naked tragedy
Wherein no filèd points are foisted in,
To make it pleasing to the ear or eye,
For simple truth is gracious enough
And needs no other points of glozing stuff.'

This, in the words of one of the greatest of them, was their aim. If they exercised imagination, they exercised it only in filling up interstices in tradition, in vivifying incident, in animating character, in analyzing emotion and passion. The materials on which they worked were of the coarsest kind. Some wretched story of calamity and crime, such as was then and is now constantly repeating itself in the lower and middle walks of life, furnished them with their plots. Thus, on the murder of a London merchant near Shooter's Hill, in 1573, was founded the anonymous tragedy of 'A Warning for Fair Women.' Thus, on the murder of a country gentleman in Kent, about 1551, was founded 'Arden of Faversham.' On a murder of peculiar atrocity, which occurred in Thames Street, Robert Yarington partially founded his 'Two Tragedies in One'; while on the murder of two children by their father at Calverley, in Yorkshire, was founded 'The Yorkshire Tragedy.' Of these plays, the earliest in point of publication, and presumably therefore the earliest in point of composition, was 'Arden of Faversham,' which was printed in 1592. The author of this most powerful play is not known. Whoever he was, he not only possessed incomparably the greatest purely dramatic genius which had revealed itself in tragedy anterior to the period of Shakspeare's mature activity, but he exercised, in conjunction with the writers of the school of which he was the representative, a very marked influence on the development of popular tragedy. Of so high an order of excellence is this drama, that many eminent critics have not hesitated to attribute it to Shakspeare. From that opinion we altogether dissent. It has no external evidence in its favour, and the internal evidence

2 o 2   appears

appears to us conclusive against it. Nothing can be more marked than the style of this play. Nothing can be more marked than the style of Shakspeare. So marked indeed is his style—his early style—his middle style—his latter style—that the merest tyro in literary criticism could never confound them with the style of any other poet. Now between the style of ' Arden' and the style of the plays which Shakspeare was writing in and before 1592, there is absolutely no resemblance at all. On the contrary, they are radically and essentially dissimilar. If, again, we turn to the characters, it is impossible not to feel how wide is the interval which separates the author of this drama from the youthful Shakspeare. Of all Shakspeare's powers the power of characterization was the slowest in developing itself; indeed, it developed itself so gradually that the successive stages in its progress may be distinctly traced in the plays which lie between what Gervinus calls the Period of Apprenticeship and about the end of 1598. Nothing, therefore, can be more unlikely than that in 1592 he should have suddenly exhibited a grasp and power in the delineation of character not unworthy of the maturity of his genius, and then as suddenly have relapsed into the immaturity and sketchiness of his early manner. To suppose that the firm strong hand which drew Alice Arden, Michael and Mosbie, was the same hand which must at the same time, or about the same time, have been faltering on the canvas of ' Titus Andronicus,' the ' Comedy of Errors,' and the ' Three Parts of Henry VI.,' is to suppose what is not merely contrary to all analogy, but simply incredible. Could the composition of ' Arden ' be assigned to a period subsequent to 1592 or 1593, the difficulty would not be so great. But to date it later is impossible. It appeared exactly as we have it now in that year. And whether it be, as Mr. Symonds surmises, the recast of an older play or an original production, one thing is clear, the hand which recast it is not the hand which recast ' The First Part of the Contention,' and ' The True Tragedy of Richard Duke of York '; while if on the other hand it be, what we have no doubt it is, an original work, it is equally clear that it could have emanated only from a master in the art of dramatic composition and realistic effect. And that in 1592 Shakspeare was most assuredly not.

We are convinced, then, that Shakspeare was not the author of 'Arden of Faversham,' but that it was the production of a powerful and original genius, the possessor of which it is now impossible to identify. Whoever he was, he occupies a foremost place in the history of pre-Shakspearian drama, not only as being the typical representative, and in all probability inaugurator

rator of a new and important school of Tragedy, but on account of the intrinsic excellence of his work, and on account of the influence which he and his school undoubtedly exercised on the dramatic activity of Shakspeare.

Such was the condition of the English drama when Shakspeare entered on his career. It had attained, as we have seen, a high point of poetical and rhetorical excellence in the hands of Marlowe and Peele. By Greene it had been brought into contact with ordinary life, but with ordinary life in its romantic aspects. The author of 'Arden of Faversham' had divorced it from poetry and romance, and taught it to become simply realistic. It remained for Shakspeare to combine, and in combining to perfect all these elements. Nothing can shake the supremacy of that mighty genius. Nothing can diminish the immense interval which in the maturity of his powers separated him from the most gifted of his predecessors and contemporaries. And yet, when we reflect on what had been accomplished during the period which we have been passing under review, it is impossible not to be struck with the extent of his indebtedness to those who preceded him. Everything had, as it were, been made ready for his advent. The tools with which he was to work had been forged; the patterns on which he was to work had been designed; the material on which he was to work had been prepared.

And now we must conclude. We look forward with pleasure to the continuation of Mr. Symonds' History, and if we offer no apology for the freedom with which we have spoken of what appeared to us to be blemishes in the first instalment of it, it is because we feel convinced that an appeal to Mr. Symonds's good sense and good taste will not be made in vain.

ART.

Art. III.—*History of Taxation and Taxes in England, from the earliest Times to the present Day.* By Stephen Dowell. 4 vols. London, 1884.

2. *A History of the Custom-Revenue in England, from the earliest Times to the Year 1827.* By Hubert Hall. 2 vols. London, 1885.

3. *L'Impôt sur le Revenu.* Par Joseph Chailley. Paris.

4. *Traité de la Science des Finances.* Par Paul Leroy-Beaulieu. 2 tomes. Paris.

5. *Local Government and Local Taxation in England and Wales.* By R. S. Wright and Henry Hobhouse. London, 1884.

THE place which taxation takes either in ordinary history or in general literature, is disproportionately small to the influence exerted by a good or a bad system of finance over both the happiness and the habits of mankind. A force which, among other results, has excited dangerous revolts, has split and severed mighty empires, has brought about the decline of kingdoms, has moulded the forms of the dwelling-places, has modified the clothes, and at times even excited the diseases of nations, must be admitted to be amongst one of the most powerful, as well as one of the most all-pervading of the influences which sway the shifting currents of human life. Yet few have been those who have devoted their time to a chronicle of the details of taxation. 'Drop by drop the cup is filled up.' The overflowings of the cup have been remembered, the bitterness of the draught has been noted, but the manner in which the drops were collected has frequently not been thought of so much moment as to deserve detailed record. We are not unmindful of the labours of earlier workers in the field, and of the merits of such books as the ' Treatise on the Principles and Practical Influence of Taxation and the Funding System,' by McCulloch, a classic of our Economic Literature ; or of the summary of the finance of this country from 1842 to 1861, contained in the ' Twenty Years of Financial Policy' of Sir Stafford Northcote, now Lord Iddesleigh. But both these able critics of our system of taxation would, it is easy to believe, have welcomed the work placed at the head of the list of books with which this article commences, the 'History of Taxation,' by Mr. Dowell. The position which Mr. Dowell holds in the office of Inland Revenue enabled him to investigate his subject to great advantage, and he has used his opportunities with great judgment. For the purpose which he contemplated, it was not a statement of principles, but a clear, straightforward chronicle of facts which was required, and such a chronicle he has given us. Mr. Dowell
takes

takes us back even as far as the times of Roman occupation of this island. But it is not till the Anglo-Saxon period that the first principle is found applied—that the justification of taxation is service rendered; in that case the defence of the country. The first tax raised in England, if we pass onward, as we may, from the exactions of the Roman conquerors, and the personal requirements of the earlier kings, was levied for a purpose as needful now as then—the defence of the country by sea. And it is curious, as showing at how early a date such a basis for taxation was thought of—that a hearth-tax—the tax of smoke-farthings, or fumage—is among the traditions of the Anglo-Saxon monarchy, going back probably even to earlier times.

No new form of taxation, Mr. Dowell mentions, resulted immediately from the Norman conquest of England. The King continued to derive his revenue mainly from the demesne. His power was increased by the confiscation of the lands of those who had fought for Harold. Gradually the necessities of the Conqueror introduced the feudal system of land-tenures. From the incidents and casualties of this, a considerable revenue was derived, practically only abolished at the outbreak of the Civil War. The roots of two other branches of modern revenue are to be traced in the obligation of all the tenants of ancient demesne to assist the King on any occasion of extraordinary expense, but more particularly on a military expedition, when the extent of their liability went even to the tenth part of their goods; and in the fact of Prisage, the right to take a cask or two casks, according to the amount of the cargo, from wine-laden ships on their arrival at a port, the rudimentary basis of customs duties may be found latent.

The feudal system, associated in poetry with a glamour of romance, with knightly bearing, with brilliant achievements, tournaments, and gay trappings, when looked at from the fiscal point of view, presents a series of transactions at least as prosaic as the entries in any shopkeeper's ledger. The tenant by knight's service was bound to serve the King personally, in arms, for forty days in every year. The description of this duty recals to the mind the host of knightly warriors, each bound to do service to his Sovereign, to undergo any hardship, to imperil his limbs, to risk his life, at the bidding of his Lord. But with the very first provision of the system of tenure all the tinsel drops off. Nothing can seem more suitable, nothing led in practice to greater acts of injustice, to more ignoble bargainings, than the system of Wardship. On the death of a tenant-in-chief, the King came in to ward off intruders until the heir appeared to claim the lands and to do homage. For this a year's profits were due. When the heir was

was a minor, and therefore incapable of doing knight-service, the King kept him in ward, and his lands in possession, providing a substitute to perform the services due from the minor. When the infant was an heiress, the King, by the same train of reasoning, was entitled to select a husband for her, and to give her away in marriage to a person capable of doing knight-service to the King. The 'maritigium,' or right of bestowal in marriage, was extended eventually to men. Thus on the Exchequer Rolls is the entry that 'Walter de Caucey gives 15*l.* for leave to marry when and whom he pleases; Wiverone, of Ipswich, 4*l.*, and a mark of silver, that she may not be married, except to her own good liking : ne capiat virum nisi quem voluerit.' Even marriage did not always completely extinguish the rights of the Sovereign in these matters : thus, 'The wife of Hugo de Nevill gives to the King 200 hens for permission to sleep with her husband, Hugo de Nevill, for one night, Thomas de Sandford being pledged for 100 hens. Robert de Abrincis fines for pardon of the King's ill-will in the matter of the daughter of Geldewin de Dol,' &c. The system of exacting fines on every possible occasion gradually extended itself. Thus, 'The Bishop of Winchester owes a tonell of good wine for not reminding the King (John) about a girdle for the Countess of Albemarle ; and Robert de Vaux fines in five of the best palfreys that the same King would hold his tongue about the wife of Henry Pinel.' * These extracts show how soon the system of fines became a mere method of arbitrary exaction. The rule of knight-service in person did not last long either. The feudal array was difficult to manage ; great barons arrived late at the muster of the host; all sorts of disputes and wranglings occurred about place and precedence ; the strict limitation of the term of compulsory service to forty days fixed an inconvenient term to any lengthened expedition. Hence Henry Plantagenet found it far more convenient, when preparing for his expedition to Toulouse, to levy a fine in money on every knight's fee, than to depend on the personal service of the barons. 'Hoc anno, 1159, rex Henricus scotugium sive scutagium de Anglia accepit.' Expressing the matter gently, King Henry—

'taking into consideration the length and difficulty of the way, and being unwilling to disturb either the knights who lived in the country or the burghers and country people generally, levied, in Normandy, sixty Angevin shillings on every knight's fee, and from all his other possessions, in Normandy, England, or elsewhere, according to that which seemed to him good, and took with him, for

---

* Dowell, vol. i. p. 28.

the expedition to Toulouse, his chief barons with a few personal followers, and an innumerable host of mercenaries.'—Rob. de Monte, Stubbs, 'Select Charters,' p. 122.

The tax was termed scutage, or shield-money. The arrangement is interesting as an early example of commutation for personal service. About the same date, the obligation of the inhabitants of the cities and towns of the kingdom to contribute to the general taxation was made to correspond more closely with that of the dwellers beyond those boundaries. When the county, including the rural tenants of demesne, yielded 'danegeld,' the citizens yielded an ' auxilium.' From this date the idea of a division between rural and urban taxation appears to have become fixed, greatly as the application of the revenue raised has varied since that period. There had, from an early date, been a tendency to tax the inhabitants of towns more heavily than the inhabitants of the country. Several causes led to this. The powerful baron was more able to resist ; the wealth of the burgher was more obvious. Against this tendency may be set the capacity of the citizens to combine, and occasionally the desire of the monarch to play off the power of the towns against that of the baronage,—hence inducing him to mitigate exactions on those whose assistance he needed most.

An obligation to pay a tax, rated according to the value of the property possessed, had been recognized in England from a very early period, but the reducing this obligation to a system is connected with the Crusades. Like the other arrangements just mentioned, this dates from the time of Henry II. The tax ' touched all movables, reaching the landowner through his cattle, farming stock, and corn, and other produce of lands, and the burgher or townsman through his furniture, money, and stock-in-trade, and was first introduced into this country on the occasion of the Saladin tithe in 1188.' *

Direct taxation, the readiest method of raising a revenue from a fiscal point of view, is open, among others, to one serious objection, by which the extreme severity of its application is fortunately checked. The method, whether the form be that of a tenth on movable property, as in the time of Henry II., or of an income-tax in more recent times, is so ready and so easy to put in practice by those who have to raise the revenue, that the draughts on those who have to find the money are apt to be prolonged and redoubled till they will bear it no longer. The scutages in the reign of Richard I. were not very numerous, nor at very high rates, and the necessity of ransoming the

---

* Dowell, vol. i. p. 44.

monarch may have reconciled his subjects to the taxation needed for that purpose. But in the reign of King John, no less than ten scutages were levied, and at an increased rate. The irritation induced by these heavy demands caused the limitation of the arbitrary power of the monarch by the strict terms of the Great Charter, which not only determined the occasions on which a scutage or aid might be levied, but provided that the prelates, earls, and barons should be summoned by personal writs, and the other tenants-in-chief by a general writ to the sheriffs and bailiffs, to take the common counsel of the realm on imposing such a tax.

The constitutional principle of the assent of the taxpayers being thus established, the next point that arose was the question of exemptions from non-liability to meet the imposition. Some exemptions to the taxation on movables had been allowed from the first. In the case of the knights, their arms, horses and clothing; in the case of the clergy, their horses, books and clothing, and vestments and church furniture of every sort, and also the jewels of clergy and laity, are the earliest instances cited, together with an exemption for those who served personally. The point of capability did not enter into consideration at the first. But when this form of taxation was universally applied, the impossibility of including the poorest classes became obvious. Hence in 1232 an exemption was granted for every man who had not movables of the kind specified to the value of forty pennies, a quarter of a mark, at least. A similar exemption was allowed in 1237, but the assessments were probably not very strictly enforced,

'For,' as Mr. Dowell mentions, 'in the following reign when, in 1275, the fourth year of Edward I., the first parliament of Westminster granted to the King a fifteenth, and the people were assessed *ud unguem, i.e.* up to the full value of property, the proceeding is characterised as unusual and unheard of, "inaudito more ad unguem taxatam;" and in the next year, 1276, the King, willing to spare the poor, granted an exemption to all who had not of the value of 15s. in goods, a considerable advance upon the exemptions from the fortieth of 1232 and the thirtieth of 1237.'—Dowell, vol. i., p. 75.

The statements as to exemptions give some curious indications of the details of personal property at various periods; thus, in the assessment of 1297, the following articles were exempted. In counties the armour, riding-horses, jewels and clothes of knights and gentlemen and their wives, and their vessels of gold, silver, and brass. In cities, boroughs, and market-towns, a suit of clothes for every man and another for his wife, a bed for both of them, a ring and a buckle of gold or silver, a girdle

of

of silk in ordinary use by them, and a cup of silver or mazer from which they drank. Everywhere, the goods of any person not amounting in the whole to 5s. in value.

Here again we find the principle of exemptions applied and extended. It is well to make these observations at the earliest point when this method of taxation was introduced, as showing that the necessity for these exemptions was recognized from the first, and further that the assessment appears to have varied to some extent in proportion to the severity of the exaction, just as an income-tax nowadays is more productive proportionally at a lower than at a higher rate. There appears to be a curiously perverted form of conscience among the majority of taxpayers, which, while causing them to be willing to submit to what they consider moderate taxation, causes them also to endeavour to evade the charge when it exceeds what seems to them right and fit to pay. People apparently will make an honest return if the rate does not exceed say threepence in the pound ; but if it is a shilling, any evasion seems excusable. And the same principle, or want of it, appears to have existed in all ages.

The taxes hitherto mentioned all fell on the inhabitants of the realm. But from a very remote period, the foreign trade of the country had been subject to a contribution.

'Another ancient source of revenue in England consisted in exactions of toll at the ports from merchants importing or exporting goods. The origin of these exactions is unknown ; but the reason for their existence is clear. The merchant in those predatory times, when every one was so ready and eager to fleece him, that "pillé comme un marchand," became subsequently a proverb, willingly paid, on entering the kingdom and on taking his merchandize out of it, toll to the king, for the necessary safeguard for himself and his merchandize, "ineundo, morando, et redeundo," in port, on land, and on the seas. The toll was, in short, in the nature of a premium paid to the King for insurance. But in whatever manner these tolls may have commenced in England, they became subsequently definite in amount, acquired by continuance the validity allowed to that which has long existed, and came to be termed " consuetudines," or customs.' —Dowell, vol. i. p. 83.

The duties levied in this manner, perhaps because they were for the most part paid by foreigners, came to be regarded more as a direct payment to the King, and under the control of his personal officers, than in the case of other taxation. Thus the prisage of wine was a toll, taken by the King's officer, of one cask from a cargo consisting of ten up to twenty casks, and of two casks from a cargo of twenty or more; and when in 1302 the King offered to commute his prisage on the wine of of the foreign merchants for a fixed charge, the duty, fixed at two shillings for every tun imported, was termed 'butlerage,' as in commutation of the rights of the King's butler. To this the foreign merchants agreed; but when in the next year, 1303, the King endeavoured to obtain the consent of his native merchants to a similar arrangement regarding his prisage of the wine imported by them, he was unable to do so. The matter was fully discussed at a meeting held in York, to which forty-two towns sent representatives; but the King's proposal was rejected. The new customs on wine and merchandize were objected to as contrary to the provisions of Magna Charta. They were suspended in 1311, but revived in 1322, reconfirmed in 1328, and received legal sanction in the Statute of the Staple in 1353. Such is the history of the foundation of the Customs' duties.

Shortly after this, the direct taxation of the country was re-arranged and placed on a basis which entirely altered the system followed, and placed it on a plan by far less objectionable, in the sense that the amount to be raised became far more certain and fixed than before. Grants had previously been made to the Crown, whether compulsory or otherwise, of the fifteenth from the counties outside the royal demesne, and the tenth from cities, towns, and demesne; but the fifteenth and tenth granted in the year 1332, though assessed and collected under writs in the ordinary form, were enforced with great strictness. Hence the tax seemed to be four times heavier than it had been before, and this gave rise to considerable complaints.

In consequence of such complaints, an arrangement was made by which a fixed sum was taken from each township as a composition for the tax. The length of time that this system has continued had better be described in Mr. Dowell's words :—

'Upon the basis of this settlement of the fifteenth and tenth in 1334, direct taxation mainly proceeded from this date until it became the practice to add to the grant of fifteenths and tenths a general subsidy on lands and goods. Changed from what the French term a *de quotité* to a tax *de répartition*, from what, had not the word in the present day a peculiar meaning, we should term a rate, to a fixed land tax, being, not the fractional grant on moveables it purported to be, but a stated sum divisible between certain districts, the tax in this form came to be regarded by the people almost as of constitutional right. When less than the sum for a full fifteenth and tenth was required, half a fifteenth or tenth was granted; and when a greater sum was required, it was granted under the name of two-fifteenths and tenths, or as the case might be. All attempts to introduce other forms of taxation or to disturb the settlement of 1334

almost

almost invariably failed. We see the dogged insistence of the Englishman in this matter prevailing in after times to turn the general subsidy or new rate of the Tudor period into another tax of a fixed sum. The parliamentary assessments of the Commonwealth times continued the tradition. And when, after the Revolution, another attempt was made to introduce and establish the principles of rating in taxation, the property tax of William III., planted in the same soil, grew gradually to resemble the assessments, the subsidies, and the fifteenths and tenths in the form it attained of the fixed land tax of the eighteenth century. To the present day, at the distance of five centuries and a half, the consequences of the arrangement made in 1334 for the local assessment of the fifteenth and tenth are clearly visible in England.'—Dowell, vol. i. p. 98.

The troubles which followed after the death of the Black Prince caused a more speedy mode of raising a revenue to be desired, and the poll-tax of 1377—'a tax hitherto unheard of'—was agreed to. This first poll-tax was levied, and paid apparently without murmuring. Perhaps the pressing danger of invasion threatened by the French rendered the people more pliable. But as troubles continued, another tax of the same description was agreed to—equally a poll-tax—but graduated so as to be less open to objection on the ground of inequality. Rank was the basis taken.

The two Dukes of Lancaster and Bretagne were charged each 10 marks, or 6*l.* 13*s.* 4*d.* Earls and Countesses, being widows, 6 marks, or 4*l.*; Barons and bannerets, 3 marks; Knights Bachelors and substantial Esquires, a mark and a half; Esquires of less estate and substantial merchants, half a mark. The Knights Hospitallers were charged separately. The Chief Prior, the same as a Baron. Every Commander of the Order, the same as a Knight Bachelor. Every other brother, being a Knight of the Order, 13*s.* 4*d.* The Judges and the Chief Baron of the Exchequer were charged 5*l.* Serjeants and grand 'apprentices of the law,' 2*l.*; every other 'apprentice to the profession of the law,' 1*l.*; all other apprentices and attorneys, 6*s.* 8*d.*

The Mayor of London was charged on the footing of an earl; the aldermen of London and the mayors of the great towns on the scale of barons; franklins, farmers, and cattle-dealers, half a mark or a quarter of a mark. For the clergy a special scale was fixed. The Archbishop of Canterbury, 6*l.* 13*s.* 4*d.*; bishops, mitred abbots, and other spiritual persons, being peers, 4*l.*; other beneficed clergy from 3*l.* down to 5*s.*, according to the value of their office; monks and nuns, according to the value of the house to which they belonged, from 3*s.* 4*d.* down to 4*d.*

This

This law was also the charge on the poorest class which paid the tax at all. The classification of the inhabitants of the realm according to the differences in this scale is curious. It places the Archbishop of Canterbury on the same footing as the dukes of the blood royal, and ranks the other bishops and mitred abbots for fiscal purposes with earls. The Mayor of London was on the same level. The Judges and the Chief Baron of the Exchequer are ranked above earls, and next to the rank on which the Archbishop is placed. While the high standing of the superior clergy is thus shown, the lower ranks among the clergy are estimated no higher than the common people, and are taxed like them. The yield of this graduated poll-tax of 1379 does not appear to have differed much from that received from the simpler arrangement of 1377 —one example out of many that over-elaborated systems of taxation rarely answer. In taxation, as in most other arrangements which concern large bodies of people, the simplest usually answers the best. When in 1380 the need arose for raising a large amount by taxation, another plan was adopted. In this arrangement, however, there was a provision by means of which it was intended that 'the rich should help the poor— the strong to help the weak.' The wealthiest was not to pay more than 60 groats, 20 shillings for himself and his wife, and no person less than a single groat for himself and his wife, that is to say, 2d. each. This tax was the proximate cause of the peasants' insurrection under Wat Tyler. The arrangement by which the strong were to help the weak had failed to ensure the popularity of the impost, founded as it was on the objectionable groat-tax of 1377, and the final outbreak of hostility to it was caused by the insolence of one of the farmers of the impost; for so difficult was the collection of the tax, that it became necessary to get in the arrears by farming them.

After this, the old method of raising what was needed by fifteenths and tenths was resumed. A graduated income-tax was, however, attempted in 1435, and again in 1450. The tax went as low as the yearly value of 1l. Those with smaller fixed incomes were exempted, as also persons holding offices, wages, or fees, for a term of years, or less than freehold, up to a value of 2l. The scale of taxation was, from 1l. to 20l., sixpence in the pound; over 20l. and including 200l., a shilling in the pound; and over 200l., two shillings in the pound. The heavy burthens, of which this income-tax was a part, formed one of the grievances which brought on the rebellion of which Jack Cade was the leader. It is somewhat singular and instructive, as showing how little in reality the effect of a tax may turn out

to

to correspond with expectation, that both these rebellions (that in which Wat Tyler and that in which Jack Cade figured as leaders) followed on attempts to adjust the incidence of taxation to the capacity of the tax-payer to meet the burden ; that is to say, to levy a tax on the progressive system. Intended to be popular, it turned out to be the reverse.

From the reign of Edward III. onwards the sums raised by means of the Customs formed a large part—at times more than half—of the revenue of the King. The natural desire to secure as much as possible from foreigners led to taxes being imposed on aliens at high rates. Thus, in the time of Edward IV. all merchants, with exceptions in favour of the merchants of Spain, Bretagne, and the merchants of the Steel Yard—merchants of Almagne, having the house in London termed Guilda Theuticorum, were charged forty shillings a year, and any alien keeping a house for the ' bruying of bere ' was charged twenty shillings. These sums, however, did not meet the requirements for Edward IV.'s extravagances. Mr. Dowell relates the manner in which he obtained assistance through the influence of the goodwill shown him individually.

' Sometimes he applied, personally, to the rich for aid ; sometimes, by letters, and sometimes by means of commissioners, in the manner used in former times for the tallages on the tenants of demesne. The first method is amusingly illustrated in the case of the benevolent widow of the well-known story. Edward, one of the handsomest men of the age until worn-out by debauchery, was, moreover, a particular favourite with the ladies; and this rich widow, when he asked her for a benevolence, gave him 20*l.* down at once, saying: "By my troth, for thy lovely countenance thou shalt have even 20*l.*" The King, who had "looked for scarce half that sum, thanked her, and lovinglie kissed her," gaining her heart and purse, for she doubled the benevolence, paying another 20*l.*, either "because she esteemed the kiss of a king so precious a jewele," or "because the flavour of his breath did so comfort her stomach."'—Dowell, vol. i. p. 156.

The power of calling on those who are, or are believed to be wealthy for assistance thus, naturally leads to great abuses. Still the raising money in this manner continued to be practised nearly a century and a half later than this date. To a popular King like Edward IV., reigning at a time when the merchants and traders were subject to a comparatively light taxation, and were rapidly increasing in wealth, and who besides ' used such gentle fashions towards them, with freendlie praier of their assistance in his necessitie, that they could not otherwise doo, but franklie and freelie yield and give him a reasonable and competent sum,' large amounts were not grudged. Much later,

later, Queen Elizabeth also received many gifts from her subjects :—

' These were offered not only by the nobility and leading gentry on New Year's Day, or other fitting occasions, but sometimes by towns collectively; and a picture of a benevolence as hearty as the grant of the first subsidy to the Queen is presented where the Mayor of Coventry gives to the Queen a handsome purse, well filled. " I have few such gifts, Mr. Mayor," the Queen says kindly; "it is a hundred pounds in gold!" "Please your Grace," replies the Mayor, "it is a great deal more we give you." " What is that ? " says the Queen. " It is," the Mayor replies, " the hearts of your loving subjects." And the Queen says, " We thank you, Mr. Mayor, it is a great deal more indeed." '—Dowell, vol. i. p. 203.

With this may be compared the money wrung by James I. from the merchant of London whom Mr. Dowell mentions. This merchant, who had been a cheesemonger, but was now rich, was sent for by the Council, and required to give the King 200*l.*, or to go into the Palatinate, and supply the army with cheese. Being eighty years of age he consented, though he had better have paid nine subsidies according to the valuation he stood at. The times were different ; what had been endured from more genial monarchs became unbearable when inflicted by the stiffer hands of the Stuarts, and in 1627 Charles I. had to give his assent to the Petition of Right, by which this form of exaction was eventually suppressed. Nearly at this last date, in 1623, three-fifteenths and tenths were granted to the King. These proved to be the last time that this form of taxation was employed. Subsidies continued in the old form for some time longer.

As taxation and not constitutional history is the subject before us, we shall not touch on the questions which open out from the decision in Bates's case, from which the Customs duties on currants depends, nor on the better known imposition of Ship-money, resisted by Hampden.

The same reason withholds us from giving more than a short reference to Mr. Hubert Hall's careful study of the History of the Custom-Revenue in England. Mr. Hall's connection with the Record Office has facilitated his researches, in the same manner that Mr. Dowell's connection with the Inland Revenue Department has given him an insight denied to the outer world. The scheme of the two books is entirely different. Mr. Hall deals with the history, we were about to say the law, while Mr. Dowell, a lawyer by profession, deals with the facts. Mr. Dowell explains that his ' work is the result of notes which, originally put together as memoranda for personal observation,

have

www.ingramcontent.com/pod-product-compliance
Lightning Source LLC
Chambersburg PA
CBHW022153020726
47496CB00008B/2692